Praise

'What has evolved over the
around leadership – is the r... ...understanding that
leadership as an "activity" is not a hierarchical right
earned based on seniority of position or job role but
one that is earned by acts of doing and behaving
from one's whole self in the most authentic of ways,
and yes, of course, combined with drawing upon
one's own experiences. This book is a great reminder
of just that, drawing, in this instance, from leaders
in music. The point of leadership and leading – it
occurs everywhere – and in all settings and walks
of life. The "art of leading" is to role model doing it
outstandingly well!'
— **Kirstie Donnelly**, MBE, Chief Executive
Officer, City & Guilds

'This book skilfully pulls together the challenges that
resonate with the leaders of today. It explores and
gets to the heart of what sits beyond the neglected
but essential acts and diagnoses practical ways to
redress these acts. There is deep appreciation for
the tensions that leaders face, while also building a
compelling case for change and a starting point to
create time for more conscious thinking, connection
and self-care. This book is a must-read for all leaders
committed to getting the best out of themselves and
their people.'
— **Jude Baliti**, Head of Partner Development,
Talent and Coaching, Big 4 Consulting Firm

'There are many valuable insights to be taken from this book, and most of them aren't rocket science – just a reminder of the basics that we often forget. The simple art of improving our attention management and focusing on getting the right things done for the right reasons can only be achieved by giving ourselves more time to think and reflect in what can be a frantic world. Taking time out to read this book will remind you of some of the habits that we really should be getting back into!'

— **Gary Shewan**, Learning and Development Business Partner, Legal & General

'This important book challenges leaders to move beyond the relentless pursuit of productivity and embrace the rhythms that sustain long-term success. Because the best leaders – like the best artists – know that the space between the notes is just as important as the notes themselves. Organisations move at the speed of trust. Take lessons from Bowie, Air and Raye!'

— **Stephen Greene**, CBE, CEO, RockCorps

'While the use of the term VUCA (volatile, uncertain, complex and ambiguous) has dropped out of regular use, it feels like that is exactly the world that leaders are operating in now. Therefore, having a structure and ideas for how to create time to understand the VUCA world, gain the trust of those that you need to work with to be successful and enable you to be resilient, is a must read. This

book sets out a series of strategies that allow you to be successful in the VUCA world and take care of yourself and your team at the same time.'
— **Noel McGonigle**, MBA, HR Director, Savills UK, Europe and Middle East

'This book lands at a moment in time when it is most needed. Like the "boiling frog" we have not adequately noticed nor addressed the growing pressures leaders face. The authors of this excellent book have noticed, and they bring real credibility as long time students of the art and practice of leadership to identify and redress areas which have too often been neglected. Inspired by music and ground-breaking creative artists, the authors bring to life enduring principles of leadership, like making time to think, building trusting relationships and the perennial challenge of self-care. I have been beautifully challenged and helped to build better leadership habits: I will take time to think – "to go slow to go fast"; I will be more trusting in order to win greater trustworthiness and I will be "properly selfish" so I am there for the people I have the privilege to lead. Thank you!'
— **Farren Drury**, MBE, Leadership and High Performance Coach

'The distillation of the latest thinking and research coupled with practical solutions make this an essential read for all leaders and those interested in leadership development. Written in an accessible style there will be something to take away in every chapter.'

— **Peter Coats**, Group Protection Academy Manager, Legal & General

The Neglected Acts of Leadership

And how music can help
you rediscover them

Andy Dent, Catrina Hewitson and Caroline Taylor

R^ethink

First published in Great Britain in 2025
by Rethink Press (www.rethinkpress.com)

Contents

Introduction

We work with and speak to hundreds of leaders each year. They are experienced, skilful, brave and determined. They are also living more hectic and fragmented lives than ever before, with concerning consequences. In the midst of crammed diaries, complex decisions, hybrid working, exponential growth in data, disruptive change and a volatile global environment, certain essential acts of leadership are going missing.

These neglected acts of leadership have nothing to do with negligence.

We've noticed a pattern of neglect happening at the same time as leaders are working harder and at higher intensity than ever before.

We are not implying that leaders are not diligent nor advocating that leaders need to do more. However, we do want to champion the idea of pausing, noticing and refocusing on fundamental aspects of leadership, taking time to rebuild a solid foundation for leadership that allows for future growth, adaptation and longevity.

The three neglected acts of leadership that we focus on in this book are:

1. Thinking time

2. Trust building

3. Time for self

When we thought about the stories we might tell to illustrate what we wanted to say about our neglected acts of leadership and what we can do about this dilemma, we found ourselves not talking about business or organisational examples. We were talking about the actions of artists and musicians.

We spoke about Air's hypnotic debut album, *Moon Safari*, and how the French duo thought carefully about the kind of music they wanted to make. They took the time to step back when they needed to, making sure their sound was exactly right.

We discussed the tales of David Bowie making *Low* – a radical shift in his musical style – and investing time to build a bond of personal trust with his co-creators before they did groundbreaking work together in Berlin.

We looked at the way Raye emerged as an independent artist and the glorious success that followed her album *My 21st Century Blues* once she stopped working seven days a week to please others and took time to become the artist she wanted to be.

We have taken these stories, which all ended in creative and commercial success, as our starting point. We hope that they will intrigue and inspire you too.

We next wanted to examine – at global, organisational and personal levels – what causes our neglected acts of leadership. What combination of phenomena creates a situation where leaders are frantically busy and yet spending less and less time on basic leadership practice? As with great albums, there are diverse influences – from slow-building social change, which means trust in authority is no longer a given, to the more recent and worrying trends like rising stress and burnout; from the disappearing boundaries between work and home to the notion of busyness as a status symbol. The picture is fascinating and relentless.

Most of the leaders we talked to as we began to develop this book were quick to agree that they didn't have sufficient time for thinking, for building trust or for time for themselves, and that they were uncomfortable with this situation. We recognise that we don't need to convince anyone that addressing these neglected acts is a good thing.

Or do we?

Even though many of those we consulted agreed with the reasonableness of what we were saying, there is emotional complexity, for example, around where leaders feel justified spending their time when there are daily fires to fight and people who need their attention. We've acknowledged this reality for each of our three neglected acts, and we have paid attention to the tensions that must be navigated before the situation changes.

Finally, we come to the action leaders can take to tackle the neglect. We have focused on suggestions that are simple to implement. They are also transformative – not only for leaders, but also for the people they work and collaborate with and the organisations they lead.

Rather like much-played lead singles, there are well-known ideas and models associated with each of our neglected acts. We believe it's time to go beyond the obvious and familiar. It's time to find solutions. It's time, crucially, to form habits that support sustainable change and, as a result, sustainable leaders.

When it comes to *time to think*, many people are asked to *be more strategic* and *take a balcony view*. We wouldn't undermine the value of either, but what does this mean you need to do in practice? Also, too many people are waiting for a perfect future moment after the new system is implemented; the new team is recruited; the intractable decisions have been made by someone, somewhere; and, finally, when there will be time to breathe and think. In practice that perfect moment never arrives.

At the moment, the conversation on repeat in organisations around *building trust* is the need to create psychological safety. It's a wonderful idea, and the benefits are well documented and robustly researched, but what's the opening track? Where do you, as an individual leader, make a start in building lasting trust?

In terms of *time for self*, we've all been talking about resilience for a long time. The wellness industry is enjoying smash-hit success, and yet how many people tune out the background noise and work out what they really need to sustain themselves, and to thrive and inspire others? Even if they've found the solution, how many people make that practice habitual?

On each of our featured albums there are moments of brilliance that are less well known – the overlooked or underrated tracks. Like them, our practical actions are there to be discovered once you sit still for a while, focus and go beyond the obvious. We believe those actions will become essential for you.

Each part of the book draws parallels between leadership acts and our inspirational musicians. It really doesn't matter if you're not a fan (although we'd definitely recommend any of our three albums to you). Music is life-enhancing, offering inspiration and insight that extend beyond conventional business wisdom. Like great leadership, the effect can be memorable and profound.

By tapping into this emotional connection, we aim to deepen your understanding of leadership and encourage you to rethink your practice. With that in mind, this book offers you the scope to pause, reflect and redefine your own leadership actions.

Throughout the book, we acknowledge the challenges leaders face and provide insights, ideas and stories to help you change your habits and make more conscious choices.

Ultimately, our goal is to encourage leaders to reclaim their potential and find renewed inspiration in their roles. By providing practical suggestions and actionable steps, we aim to help people navigate the complexities of modern leadership with confidence and clarity.

We want to help you build better relationships and also take back that most precious of commodities: time. Let's face it – any leader who operates with the hopeful notion that at some future point there will be a right time to pause and think has a problem. In reality, *that's never going to happen.*

We invite you to take time to discover for yourself how to reverse these neglected acts of leadership and to reconnect with the power of thinking time, trust building and time for yourself.

PART ONE
THE NEGLECT OF THINKING TIME

1
The Story Of
Moon Safari By Air

The French band's name Air is an acronym of *amour, imagine, rêve* (love, imagine, dream). The band formed in 1995, when French popular music had a thriving electronic dance scene, including the internationally successful Daft Punk.

Air comprised a duo of unconventional musicians. Its founders, Nicolas Godin and Jean-Benoît Dunckel, studied architecture and mathematics, respectively. Having considered the music environment and the technology available to them that 'meant you could make cool music without being a rocker', they set out to a create a distinctive electronic sound.[1]

---

1   G Palladev, 'Air – Moon Safari. Story behind the album. Track by track guide' (Medium, 15 August 2022), https://medium.com/@palladev/air-moon-safari-story-behind-the-album-track-by-track-guide-40a0df366c57, accessed 17 November 2024

When Air emerged with *Moon Safari* in the late nineties, clubgoers had come to expect French bands to produce great dance tunes, but this wasn't the arena Air wanted to compete in. Instead, they decided to produce music that people listened to on Sunday mornings, after spending Saturday nights on the dance floor.

That was a bold and deliberate choice. From the beginning, the band members took time to think about who and how they wanted to be and, in so doing, differentiate themselves from their peers. Both artists were great theatre goers, and their musical influences were diverse, eclectic and surprising, drawn from astrophysics, technology, Rachmaninov, The Beatles, cinema soundtracks and TV shows (including *Charlie's Angels*, the inspiration for their track 'Kelly Watch the Stars').

What emerged was their own innovative style, which resisted the standard verse–chorus structure of popular music. Beth Hirsch, who contributed vocals to the album, observed:

> 'The making of *Moon Safari* was very slow. The guys knew that they had to make the record their way. I remember them saying there was a lot of pressure on them to get it done as quickly as possible, but they resisted and did it on their terms.'[2]

---

2   Ibid.

Taking time to think was key to Air's strategy and, ultimately, to the album they created. Godin and Dunckel reflected on the genre-spanning ideas that stimulated them and developed a clear view on the music they wanted to make. They weren't afraid to take time to explore and experiment in the pursuit of excellence and fulfilment, despite pressure from their record label to produce a quick and commercial result.

Even in moments of tension, the music duo understood the power of stepping back. When recording part of *Moon Safari* at Abbey Road, they became overwhelmed with the occasion and felt unable to speak to the string players about what they needed. In the normal practice of 'busyness', especially in the expensive, highly pressured facility of the recording studio, the typical reaction might have been to carry on and to thrash out the tracks, regardless.

Air broke the convention. For them the better choice was to take time out and retreat to the countryside house of their producer (all credit to him too for suggesting this), where they took time to think, talk and reflect on where they were. After the weekend, they returned to the studio and were ready to perform. The string sections on the album are beautiful and perfect for the impact they wanted. 'He [their producer] helped us to overcome our shyness and make something massive and expressive,' said Jean-Benoît Dunckel.[3]

When *Moon Safari* was released in January 1998, Air's quirky look and sounds caught the music public's imagination. The musicians had been true to their vision and strategic plan in producing music that they hoped people would listen to on a Sunday morning.

It paid off. Within one month of its release, Air's debut album was met with universal critical acclaim; and over the course of the year, it won more plaudits and accolades.

Air's approach wasn't the easy option of turning out formulaic electronic dance hits. They relied on their own unique sense of melody and tone to create ambient tracks that sounded like nothing else. On the twenty-fifth anniversary of the release of *Moon Safari*, Liz Itkowsky said on the Albumism website:

> 'Since *Moon Safari*, I often find myself seduced
> by the innate "coolness" that can be found
> in most things French. But that imaginary
> bar for "cool" has been set by Air. Dunckel
> and Godin wrote earnest lyrics and created

---

3   D Simpson, 'How we made Air's Moon Safari' (*The Guardian*, 31 May 2016), www.theguardian.com/culture/2016/may/31/how-we-made-moon-safari-air-jean-benoit-dunckel-nicolas-godin-interview, accessed 27 October 2024

a high-concept, theatrical album about outer space.'[4]

Itkowsky went on to praise the authenticity of the musicians' delivery as well as their conviction and creativity, saying that their respect for a wide range of genres and generations sets them apart from other musicians. She claimed *Moon Safari* to be the result of the pure dedication of two deeply passionate musicians. We're inclined to agree.

What we can learn from Air about thinking time

We take three insights from Air's use of thinking time.

1. **Incorporating thinking time before and during their work on Moon Safari was of immense value.** This included defining who and what they wanted to be as a band; departing from established musical templates; identifying who they could collaborate with; and, crucially, developing a strategic plan for their music that would differentiate them and make the album a global success. According to SoundGym, this

---

4   L Itkowsky, 'Air's Debut Album "Moon Safari" Turns 25' (Albumism, 13 January 2023), https://albumism.com/features/air-debut-album-moon-safari-album-anniversary, accessed 27 October 2024

amounted to over two million sales of *Moon Safari* worldwide.[5]

2. **They recognised the moments when they needed to step back.** They gave themselves space to breathe, think and prepare, and they also knew when they could work fast and instinctively. One of the album's biggest hits, 'Sexy Boy', began when Godin played a short riff to Dunckel, who immediately came up with the lyric, after which they laid down the track there and then. They instantly felt it worked, even the title (note: not 'Sexy Girl'), despite their initial concern that the label wouldn't approve it.

3. **They built a group of trusted collaborators.** These people were supportive, believed in the musicians' potential and were happy to share and develop their own talents in Air's orbit.

We will talk more about the power of building trust later in the book.

For now, we invite you – whether your leadership emerges through groundbreaking music, corporate life, public service, small business or entrepreneurship – to consider that time to think is no longer something you can afford to neglect.

---

5   'Air – Moon Safari' (SoundGym blog, 24 November 2020), www.soundgym.co/blog/item?id=air-moon-safari, accessed 27 October 2024

2
Why We Neglect Thinking Time

When we talk about the neglect of thinking time, we mean time for leaders to think in a way that is:

- Deeper

- More exploratory

- Reflective

- Less frantic

- Far beyond the moment, into the future

We mean the thinking time that allows you to contemplate the challenges, opportunities and complexities that lie ahead of you and to work out how to respond.

This is about the space in which new solutions and ideas come through, where you move past easy assumptions, question the status quo and imagine alternatives. Where you have the moments of clarity about what you can do to realise future potential. The chance to spend time in the calmer space in which your leadership skills are fully primed to prevent crises because you plan ahead, remove the combustibles and invest in the relationships and networks you need.

It also includes thinking time for yourself – deliberate moments when you can reflect on your experiences and recognise you can gain learning and insight that can make you stronger, wiser and more effective for the next time.

How does that sound?

This kind of thinking time should be an integral part of any leader's regular and legitimate activity. Most leaders agree with us – in principle, at least. When asked if they'd like more thinking time, they respond resoundingly with *Yes!* Nobody disagrees with us that more time to think is essential. So why is thinking time a neglected leadership act?

In this chapter we outline the global, organisational and personal phenomena that we see distract leaders from thinking time. Following that, we explore the tensions that make it difficult to take time to think, even though the arguments for doing so are clear and persuasive.

In the face of these realities, we then propose practical solutions – the starting point or the obvious lead single, like the infectiously catchy 'Sexy Boy' from *Moon Safari* – and some fresh ideas that we think deserve more attention.

Throughout, our challenge to you is to rethink thinking time and to make it a habitual activity, not a neglected one. You don't need permission to take thinking time (except perhaps from yourself?).

Where we are now

We are not making the argument that leaders don't think. Far from it.

The leaders we meet and work with are constantly thinking. They think about what people need from them during back-to-back meetings, reacting in the face of fast-flowing new information, making quick decisions, calculating and recalculating their priorities as they try to work out which fires to fight – and all before they return to their digital devices to think about how many emails they can reply to or missed calls they can return in the five minutes before their next engagement.

Does that sound familiar?

It's no wonder many leaders struggle to carve out thinking time, despite recognising its importance.

The challenge of finding time to think isn't new. Theodore Roosevelt, the twenty-sixth president of the USA (from 1933 to 1945) was known for his boundless energy and enthusiasm. He was a prolific writer, a skilled politician and an outdoorsman, yet biographies often describe him as struggling to find quiet moments for reflection due to the constant demands of his role.

In her pioneering book, *Time to Think*, Nancy Kline recognised the vital role leaders play in creating what she called 'the Thinking Environment'.[6] She set out in detail the ten components involved:

1. **Attention:** Giving people your full attention, listening without interruption

2. **Equality:** Treating everyone's thinking as equally valuable

3. **Ease:** Creating a relaxed environment where people feel at ease to think

4. **Appreciation:** Appreciating people's thinking and encouraging them

---

6   N Kline, *Time to Think: Listening to ignite the human mind* (Cassell Illustrated, 1999)

5. **Encouragement:** Encouraging exploration of ideas and possibilities

6. **Feelings:** Acknowledging and respecting emotions

7. **Information:** Providing relevant information to support thinking

8. **Diversity:** Valuing diverse perspectives and experiences

9. **Incisive questions:** Asking open-ended questions that provoke deeper thinking

10. **Place:** Choosing a physical space conducive to thinking

For us the ten components are as relevant and valuable as when Nancy Kline first articulated them. It is the likelihood of achieving some, never mind all, of these conditions that seems more remote today.

Meg Wheatley, whose book *Turning to One Another* included a chapter titled 'Am I willing to reclaim time to think?'[7], wrote on her website:

'Whether we're in a small village or a major global corporation, in any country and in any type of work, we are being asked to work faster, more competitively, more selfishly,

---

7   MJ Wheatley, *Turning to One Another: Simple conversations to restore hope to the future* (Berrett-Koehler, 2009)

and to focus only on the short-term. These values cannot lead to anything healthy and sustainable, and they are alarmingly destructive.'[8]

Referring to his 2024 New York Times Bestseller, *Slow Productivity: The lost art of accomplishment without burnout*, Cal Newport recognises a similar phenomenon:

'Our current definition of "productivity" is broken. It pushes us to treat busyness as a proxy for useful effort, leading to impossibly lengthy task lists and ceaseless meetings. We're overwhelmed by all we have to do and on the edge of burnout, left to decide between giving into soul-sapping hustle culture or rejecting ambition altogether.'[9]

As one of our clients commented, 'Every year we imagine things can't possibly become more intense than last year. And then they do.'

In this frenetic context, our brains are working, assessing, responding and surviving, though not necessarily fully functioning.

---

8   MJ Wheatley, 'Now is the time' (Margaret J Wheatley), www.margaretwheatley.com/articles/whyIwrotethebook.html, accessed 27 October 2024

9   C Newport, *Slow Productivity: The lost art of accomplishment without burnout* (Cal Newport, 2024), https://calnewport.com/slow-uk, accessed 27 October 2024

In his 2012 book, *Thinking Fast and Slow*, the Nobel laureate Daniel Kahneman referred to a *slow* way of thinking – *System 2* thinking – which is deliberate, conscious, logical, free of bias.[10]

It is this style of thinking that we believe is in grave danger of being lost.

The global perspective

Every decade has distinctive crises, and current times offer no exception.

A sense of permanent and urgent crisis

The third decade of the twenty-first century opened during a global pandemic – the first since the influenza epidemic of 1918. At the time of writing, the decade has so far been characterised by intensifying concerns about the environment, floods, earthquakes, forest fires, political division and instability, economic uncertainty and bitter wars erupting from long-standing conflicts. All played out on twenty-four-hour news cycles, with press agencies eager to report on the next disaster, followed by the next, and the next. Added to the mix is the rise of multiple new media platforms such as blogs, podcasts, influencers and other commercial models, all of which rely on clickbait. With the

---

10   D Kahneman, *Thinking, Fast and Slow* (Penguin, 2012)

concept of 'fake news', we're never quite sure of the reliability of what we're reading, and the discordant noise is deafening. It's no wonder our sense of crisis is ever present.

An easier option might be not to think about all that complexity and stay busily distracted by the buzz of the immediate day-to-day agenda.

All questions and no right answers

In the context of this turbulence, the business and organisational world feels highly ambiguous. Added to the weight of ongoing turbulence is a further dilemma – that looking at the future (for us, a core part of any leader's role) leads to more questions than answers.

Let's examine some of the questions the organisations we work with are grappling with and how complex the answers might be.

What will the world of work look like in the future, and what skills will become essential?

The World Economic Forum 'Future of Jobs Report 2023' reports that:

- Employers estimate that 44% of workers' skills will be disrupted in the next five years.

- 60% of workers will require training before 2027, but only half of workers are seen to have access to adequate training opportunities today.

- The skills that companies report to be increasing in importance the fastest (AI and big data, leadership and social influence) are not always reflected in corporate upskilling strategies.[11]

How will organisations be transformed, stay relevant and find innovative ways to add value or risk becoming obsolete?

New categorisations of customers and employees (Gens X, Y and Z, Millennials, and – hot on their heels – Generation Alpha) leave leaders facing confusion as to who is who and what different groups want from their products, services and workplaces.

This is further complicated by the fact that most people in each category would say the first thing they want is *not* to be placed in a category.

Deloitte's '2023 Gen Z and Millennial Survey' offers us some insight.[12] One of the findings quoted is that

---

11 World Economic Forum, *Future of Jobs Report 2023* (World Economic Forum, May 2023), www3.weforum.org/docs/WEF_Future_of_Jobs_2023.pdf, accessed 27 October 2024

12 Deloitte, *2023 Gen Z and Millennial Survey – Waves of change: acknowledging progress, confronting setbacks* (Deloitte, 2023), www.deloitte.com/content/dam/Deloitte/global/Documents/deloitte-2023-genz-millennial-survey.pdf, accessed 27 October 2024

'Many Gen Zs and millennials make career decisions based on their values and want to be empowered to drive change within their organizations.'

Where will our energy come from, and how is it possible to pursue growth and act with environmental and social responsibility?

In 2024 Our World in Data shared an article we recommend as an insightful read. It notes that we currently consider a wide range of energy mixes, including coal, oil, gas, nuclear, hydropower, solar, wind and biofuels. Two centuries ago, we had comparatively homogenous energy mixes, and the transition between different sources has been incredibly slow.[13]

How will geopolitics evolve over the next twenty years, and which nations and economies will thrive?

A 2022 report issued by Goldman Sachs forecast that global growth would slow then gradually decline after 2029.[14] The report also looks further ahead to even more profound change:

---

13 H Ritchie and P Rosado, 'Energy Mix – Explore global data on where our energy comes from, and how this is changing' (Our World in Data, July 2020), https://ourworldindata.org/energy-mix, accessed 27 October 2024

14 'The global economy in 2075: Growth slows as Asia rises' (Goldman Sachs, 8 December 2022), www.goldmansachs.com/insights/articles/the-global-economy-in-2075-growth-slows-as-asia-rises, accessed 27 October 2024

'Looking out to 2075, the prospect of rapid population growth in the likes of Nigeria, Pakistan, and Egypt imply that – with the appropriate policies and institutions – these economies could become some of the largest in the world.'[15]

How will AI, quantum computing and other technologies impact businesses organisations, humans and the planet?

In an Emerging Technologies article from Davos 2024, leaders called for 'measured, thoughtful and inclusive conversations that consider the intricate interplay between technology, governance and societal well-being'.[16]

With globally significant, intractable questions like this to grapple with, it's increasingly apparent that we live in a world where there are few clear – and even fewer right – answers. To complicate matters further, the essential values, principles and ethics we might use to guide us can be as divisive as the questions themselves.

Given the huge scale of these dilemmas, perhaps it's easier to stay focused on the things we can do with

---

15 Ibid.
16 J Jurgens, 'AI and emerging technology at Davos 2024: 5 surprising things to know' (World Economic Forum, 26 January 2024), www. weforum.org/stories/2024/01/surprising-things-to-know-about-ai- and-emerging-technology-at-davos-2024, accessed 27 October 2024

some certainty – work on the next quarter, attend our scheduled meetings without question, wade through this week's to-do list. There's a comfort and sense of purpose in working, in what Stephen Covey would call our *circle of control*, but it doesn't help us lift our eyes to the horizon and take a good look.[17]

Information overload

In the heat and confusion, a further complication is that tackling any of these questions needs not just the nuanced, emotionally intelligent conversations dreamed of at Davos.[18] The ability to interpret vast and increasing amounts of data and stay open to diverse perspectives is also required.

In other words, we need the best thinking our brains are capable of. We need the brain power that can explore paradoxes, spark creativity, exercise fine judgement, design solutions and practice empathy, and to muster the energy to reflect on and learn from our experiences.

We live in an atmosphere, though, that mitigates against our individual and collective brains doing this kind of thinking. Many of us would recognise that we exist with or are in danger of cognitive overload, plugged in as we are to virtual meetings, email,

---

17 SR Covey, *The 7 Habits of Highly Effective People: Powerful lessons in personal change* (Simon & Schuster, 2013)
18 Ibid.

instant messaging, online information, smart devices, rapid incoming events and social media. It's all accessible twenty-four hours per day, connecting us to volumes of information and stimulus that our brains have no hope of processing effectively.

In addition, our consumption of information tends to be fragmented. Picture a typical morning: new information, shared on a detailed Excel spreadsheet on screen, is interrupted by glances at your second screen to check if your emails are piling up. You then jump onto a rapid Teams call because someone spotted a space in your diary. Throughout this, your phone constantly pings with notifications that persuade you to scroll through LinkedIn for five minutes before returning your attention to an actual, 3D team member standing beside your desk who would love a word with you.

In this onslaught of data and distraction, we are in danger of decreased productivity, feeling overwhelmed, lack of focus, loss of perspective and faulty decision making. Beyond that, we face strained relationships, exhaustion and anxiety.

In this situation we risk moving into what psychiatrist Jud Brewer described in the *Harvard Business Review* as 'the anxiety–distraction feedback loop'.[19] An example

---

19 J Brewer, 'Are you stuck in the anxiety-distraction feedback loop?' (*Harvard Business Review*, 19 May 2020), https://hbr.org/2020/05/are-you-stuck-in-the-anxiety-distraction-feedback-loop, accessed 27 October 2024

might be that we have fallen into the habit of scrolling through social media sites as a momentary relief from the intensity of the working day. The repetition and familiarity reassure and calm us, even if the content is irritating or irrelevant. The more we repeat the process as a response to pressure, the more compelling the content becomes. It's so much easier than taking time to tackle a question we have no way of knowing the answer to or attempting a conversation with an uncertain outcome.

CASE STUDY: The disadvantage of distractions

Ali was a highly action-orientated senior leader in his early forties. He was a self-professed 'doer', which helped him secure several internal promotions for his decisiveness and hands-on approach.

His days were now meant for strategic thinking – poring over market reports, analysing trends, competitor intelligence – and turning this insight into opportunities and future organisational strategy.

Instead, he often found himself flitting between his overflowing inbox or getting distracted by LinkedIn notifications, which inexplicably pulled him into unproductive scrolling and browsing.

He would often look perplexed at the clock. He had put time aside for strategic exploration but had nothing to show for it but a slightly less full inbox and a couple of likes and comments on LinkedIn.

Taking time for the big, messy leadership challenges ahead requires much more:

- Conscious, effortful thinking
- Breaking out of unfamiliar patterns
- Stepping into the unknown

It's scary, and so we distract ourselves again.

The organisational perspective

Having explored the global phenomena that steal, impair and cause us to avoid our thinking time, we turn to organisational life to examine the contributory factors we discover there.

Working one step down

The authors of the 2017 book *Extreme Ownership: How US Navy Seals train and win* say that as a leader, if you are planning the details together with your team, you will have the same perspective as them, which adds little value. If you let them plan the details, it allows them to own their piece of the plan.[20]

---

20 J Willink and L Babin, *Extreme Ownership: How US Navy Seals train and win* (St. Martin's Press, 2017)

This is wise advice from two former US Navy Seals. We'd ask you to think about how often your schedule leaves you feeling that you're down in the weeds. Is your focus one step down from where it should be because your day is consumed by responding in the moment? Or is it easier not to delegate because it's faster for you to get the job done yourself?

We hear leaders say that this is their reality. They often add that it's actually a temporary phase brought about because, post-Covid, their organisation experienced leakage of key personnel, or because there's another change that demands their attention. They might say they just need to get their current project over the line or get to year end, and then miraculously, a clean and clear diary will emerge, allowing them to be forward-thinking, strategic, zen.

The problem is that this perfect zen state *never* materialises.

Perhaps you recognise that scenario? The risk of falling into a trap where you operate in a more limited version of your leadership role, spending too much time on the detail that shouldn't be within your direct domain?

There are pressures and prejudices that trap organisations *and* their people in this limit cycle. The pressures include:

- Short-term targets

- Continuous change

- Skills shortages

- Processes, systems and structures that are not fit for purpose

Examples of the prejudices are:

- Having a natural bias for being busy

- Being reluctant to delegate

- Having a reticence to admit leaders have developed a set of unhelpful day-to-day habits that are hard to shake

There is also the lingering power of busyness as a status symbol, identified by Adam Waytz, who shares the story of 'a man who immigrated to the United States and soon came to believe that the word "busy" meant "good" because when he asked people, "How are you doing?" they often responded, "Busy."'[21]

Perhaps these prejudices are so hard to shake because they keep us safe, protecting us from taking personal and organisational risks with uncertain outcomes.

---

21 A Waytz, *The Power of Human – How our shared humanity can help us create a better world* (WW Norton & Company, 2019)

We'll explore these dichotomies and what we might do about them in our next chapter. Meanwhile, in organisations everywhere…

Back-to-back meetings culture

The Covid pandemic changed how organisations worked. Where would many businesses and organisations be now, had they not been able to make use of virtual meeting platforms that kept so many people connected and able to work from the safety of their homes?

There were consequences to this leap into the virtual world. A Harvard Business School study of 3.1 million people in sixteen global cities concluded that, in the early months of the pandemic:

- Working days lengthened by an average of forty-eight minutes.

- Employees attended 13% more meetings with 14% more people in them.

- People sent 5.2% more emails, addressed to 2.9% more recipients, 8.3% of which were sent after business hours.[22]

---

22 D Kost, 'You're right! You are working longer and attending more meetings' (Harvard Business School, 14 September 2020), https://hbswk.hbs.edu/item/you-re-right-you-are-working-longer-and-attending-more-meetings, accessed 27 October 2024

As flexible and hybrid working have become the post-pandemic norm, there are unresolved questions about what the conventions for this reset of our ways of working should be. The number of meetings we attend is no longer limited to the places we can physically be, and electronic diaries mean that appointments can land in schedules without warning. It's exhausting.

Microsoft research estimates that there was a 153% increase in time spent in meetings, and a 46% increase in meetings overlapping, between 2020 and 2022.[23] This results in more pressure on leaders to be constantly available and to somehow find more time to be available than they actually have. There simply isn't enough time in the working day, so we take work home.

In addition to the technology-enabled scale of this increase, there is the human factor of FOMO (fear of missing out) at play. *What happens if I miss the essential piece of information, the game-changing conversation, the chance to make an impression on a new stakeholder?*

Another *Harvard Business Review* article, from 2024, suggests that it's not uncommon for managers to

---

23 Microsoft, 'Hybrid work is just work. Are we doing it wrong?' (Microsoft Work Trend Index Special Report, 22 September 2022), www.microsoft.com/en-us/worklab/work-trend-index/hybrid-work-is-just-work, accessed 27 October 2024

continue thinking about their job even after the official workday is over.[24]

This may involve ruminating about an issue with an employee, trying to think of a solution to a client problem, or creating a mental to-do list for the next day. The article explains that this tendency likely isn't beneficial, particularly for people new to a leadership role. In fact, constant rumination leads managers to be more depleted and less able to show up as leaders – something their employees can pick up on.

As highlighted in *Psychology Today*, even if you want to devote some time to thinking, an entire morning of meetings will consume your capacity for creativity and the ability to step beyond automatic, assumption-based patterns of thought.[25] It's a regime that literally eliminates the capacity to think.

It's clear that our prevalent meeting culture not only sucks up the time when we could be thinking, but it also impairs our capacity to think effectively, even if we are disciplined at carving out space in our agendas.

---

24 RE Jenning et al., 'Want to be a better leader? Stop thinking about work after hours' (*Harvard Business Review*, 3 January 2024), https:// hbr.org/2024/01/want-to-be-a-better-leader-stop-thinking-about-work-after-hours, accessed 27 October 2024

25 P Reed, 'The dangers of back-to-back digital meetings' (*Psychology Today* blog, 25 June 2023), www.psychologytoday.com/gb/blog/ digital-world-real-world/202306/the-dangers-of-back-to-back-digital-meetings, accessed 30 October 2024

How many of these back-to-back meetings do you really need to attend? Or do you never have time to think about that question?

Move fast and break things

The *move fast and break things* approach to creative destruction in product – and, ultimately, organisational – development gained prominence when Mark Zuckerberg highlighted it in 2009 as integral to Facebook's way of working.

Given the stratospheric success of Facebook, the concept was influential as a mindset and a practice. Organisations and individuals sought to quickly identify and learn from failures or shortcomings to iterate and improve their approach as fast as possible. With an emphasis on experimentation, rapid feedback loops and agility in decision making, the dream was to achieve better outcomes.

The benefits are attractive:

- Higher risk-to-reward ratio
- More space to innovate
- A stimulating working environment

It's the opposite approach to that used by Air when they recognised they lacked the confidence needed to talk to the string section at Abbey Road during the recording of *Moon Safari*. Instead of rapid experiments, the musicians stepped back, retreated for the weekend and gave themselves thinking time. When they came back, they were ready to collaborate and create something extraordinary.

In 2014 Facebook adapted their 'move fast and break things' mantra to 'move fast with stable infrastructure'.[26] However, according a 2014 *Business Insider* article,

> '"It doesn't (have the same ring to it),"
> Zuckerberg admitted, "which I think is
> partially why it hasn't caught on externally.
> But by building a stable infrastructure, we
> allow ourselves to always make sure that we're
> moving forward, even if we move a little bit
> slower upfront."'[27]

More than a decade, later, there's a danger that Facebook's more mature approach still hasn't caught on externally. The influence of *move fast and break things* lingers, reinforcing the idea that leadership thinking should run at a fast pace, making accelerated progress in the face of higher unpredictability, constantly moving and focusing on quick choices in the moment.

---

26 N Statt, 'Zuckerberg: "Move fast and break things" isn't how Facebook operates anymore' (CNET, 30 April 2014), www.cnet.com/tech/mobile/zuckerberg-move-fast-and-break-things-isnt-how-we-operate-anymore, accessed 30 October 2024

27 D Baer, 'Mark Zuckerberg explains why Facebook doesn't "move fast and break things" anymore' (*Business Insider*, 2 May 2014), www.businessinsider.com/mark-zuckerberg-on-facebooks-new-motto-2014-5, accessed 30 October 2024

Of course, in the right context and culture, the approach is effective. Air wrote 'Sexy Boy' from *Moon Safari* in minutes, instinctively knowing the potential of one great hook. Imperfect action beats paralysis, and building momentum via experimentation is engaging and creative.

Our observation, though, is that this way of working is less powerful when there is no counterbalance – no time to observe, reflect and learn, and to apply insight from learning to even better performance. Or when the seduction of action in the moment means reduced attention to longer-term strategy, clear direction and purpose.

There's a risk that thinking is squeezed out of the equation when it ought to be carefully integrated and protected. All heat but no light has a short-term impact at best.

Beyond this, there is a danger that time to think is perceived as less legitimate and less productive, and that leaders should rush through agenda items as quickly as possible at the expense of higher-quality conversation and outcomes. It gives rise to the finger-snapping cliché *Don't come to me with problems – bring me solutions*. This in an environment where problems are, as we have highlighted, increasingly complex, the solutions are not obvious, and we may benefit from time to ponder, ask questions, collaborate and talk to others with different points of view.

The personal perspective

Do you believe you could better serve yourself, your colleagues and your business if you could legitimise thinking time?

With the risk that organisations and organisational cultures are pushing out thinking time, how are individuals coping and responding?

'Be more strategic?'

We often hear from newly promoted managers, directors and heads of departments that their boss has told them they need to *be more strategic*.

It can feel like a defining moment – an indication to those leaders that their status has been elevated. Exciting as it may sound, they also tell us it's disconcerting. After all, they may attribute their success to date to the fact that they were great at *doing*, and now there's a new expectation based on *being*. As a result, confusion arises:

- What exactly does being more strategic mean?

- How will they as leaders manage that transition into becoming more strategic?

- What is involved exactly? Should they adapt their habits, behaviours and, in many cases, preferences?

- How can they be certain that being rather than doing will be valued?

To exacerbate the dilemma, it was until this point easy for an employer to measure the successful outcomes of what they as leaders did. The outputs of thinking and taking a strategic view are much harder to evaluate, and they are usually judged at some point in the future rather than with the instant gratification of the moment.

The most affected and concerned can be leaders who are invited into a world of ambiguity and uncertainty as a result of the competence, knowledge and ability they demonstrated in their previous role. Now they need to learn something new, almost as if starting from scratch.

There's further discomfort for anyone who has made their reputation and honed their experience working in depth and is now expected also to be adept at breadth because they sit within a leadership team. They face grappling with issues that they don't have an expert view on, and even though they may have a valid perspective to propose and great questions they could ask, they lack the confidence to do so.

When *being more strategic* leads to discomfort or, more fundamentally, questions about our sense of self and the value we bring, it's not surprising that the established *doing* default is the more attractive option.

As one of our clients said, 'If I stop doing what I did before and delegate everything to my team, what am I for?'

However, while your boss might not precisely define being more strategic, they are unlikely to be impressed by your being frantically busy. From their perspective, that might only make you appear disorganised or indecisive, particularly if they are waiting – and waiting – for you to give your interpretation of strategic priorities, offer fresh ideas, anticipate and mitigate risks, work out how to be more efficient, and plan succession in your team.

We acknowledge that it's incredibly difficult to make time and space for thinking time, given the global, organisational and personal influences that impact our environment, mindset, mood and choices. Where to start?

Do we learn from Air and their *Moon Safari* story that it is vital to set out with a clear vision, resisting external pressures and taking the time to do what feels right with determination and focus, and with the support of the right collaborators? If only it were that simple. Making and taking time to think sounds so straightforward, and we do have some practical proposals to help correct the neglect, but there are some realities to face and paradoxes to resolve before we start.

Let's examine them in our next chapter.

3
Making Time To Think: Three Tensions

In the previous chapter we considered the global, organisational and personal reasons that cause leaders to neglect thinking time. We pictured the environment, filled with cacophonous noise, that distracts us and drains the best of our brains, leaving us no space to breathe. We hesitate about being more strategic and we attach value both to busyness and to ourselves as being busy (and therefore surely important and indispensable) people. All this drives us to keep our attention focused on the now.

The more senior you are, though, the more your organisation, its executive team and your boss hold you accountable for shaping – not just reacting to – the future. It's what you're paid for. As one of our clients told us when we were designing a change management programme for their leadership population, 'We need this group of people to be on the front foot, not constantly on the receiving end of and reacting to change as it happens.' Also, as we have described, so many of the leaders we work with are convinced of the logic and necessity of time to think.

Why is it so difficult to make time to think

Surely, even in the face of demanding agendas and short-term pressure, it should be possible to block out some time in the diary, turn down the volume and begin?

In our experience, it's more complicated than that, and we've identified a series of the main three tensions at play that prevent leaders from taking that first concrete and constructive step, as outlined below.

Tension 1: To think or to do

How will anything get done if I'm always over here thinking?

When their teams are drowning in work, leaders tell us they feel guilty – even self-indulgent – if they take time away. It's a *limit cycle*. Leaders remain ever present in case their teams need support, decisions, organisational knowledge or the removal of blockages. Team members become accustomed to having constant access to leaders and view them as the primary source of everything.

In this scenario your leadership impact is instant. You have a unique and pivotal role, serving as the linchpin for your team's achievements and outcomes. No one can do what you do.

We have a belief that everyone who comes to work wants to do a good job. Why then, when you can see the difference you make by staying in the centre of your team, would you want to disrupt this pattern of behaviour? To complicate things further, sometimes you're right to be there.

This brings us to our next tension.

Tension 2: When to think and when to do

Should I drive action in the moment or contemplate essential questions about the future?

We've been influenced by Ronald Heifetz, Alexander Grashow and Marty Linksy's work on adaptive leadership at the Harvard Kennedy School of Government.[28] They use the metaphor of leaders being *on the dance floor* – in the midst of the action – and then moving

---

28 R Heifetz et al., *The Practice of Adaptive Leadership: Tools and tactics for changing your organization and the world* (Harvard Business Review Press, 2009)

deliberately to the balcony, where a broader, longer view is possible.

The dance floor is the space for the busyness of the day to day. It's the space where you work *in* the organisation as opposed to *on* it. You live in the high-pressure moments, reacting to one challenge here, reprioritising there; or at a moment's notice, stepping in because of an unexpected crisis. This busyness can become addictive and distracting.

Heifetz, Grashow and Linksy advocate moving from the dance floor to the balcony as a vital leadership practice. The perspective from the balcony enables leaders to see what's coming towards them from a distance, and to observe patterns and systems in their environment.

There's power in that perspective. It's an opportunity to interrogate existentially important issues and questions, some of which we've touched on previously:

- What is the increasing potential of AI and other technologies in organisations?
- What are the options for reducing your environmental footprint?
- How do you stay relevant and avoid obsolescence?
- How can you differentiate yourself from your competitors?

- Who are your competitors and collaborators now, and who might they be in the future?

You may not be able to answer any of those questions neatly, but you might identify scenarios, options and possibilities that you can explore further or even allocate resource to exploring.

Closer to home, the balcony view might help loosen the organisational knots that stop progress. Recent issues that our clients have described to us but never quite had time and space to tackle include:

- Why are our head office and regional structure at odds rather than working as one coherent organisation?

- What is happening in our culture and associated behaviours that mean we're using only 20% of the potential of our expensive new CRM system?

- Why do our new recruits in their twenties stay with us for less than two years?

- Why do we have ten different forms for performance management?

It makes sense to commit leadership time to those questions. This provides a different way of applying and benefitting from the in-depth skills and knowledge that we've built over time. Procrastinating on future issues, until they become urgent rather than important, risks robbing us of choices and turns the heat up as we grapple for solutions.

We also need to acknowledge that there are times when the dance floor is exactly the right place for you to be. On the dance floor, if you're an observant leader, you can gain live insight and understanding of the context you, your team and your colleagues operate in. It's a place where great, spontaneous conversations with team members happen that help build trust and understanding. People feel heard and seen by you, and your presence and visibility have a positive effect on the quality of the work environment. In that moment, you may be *exactly* the right person to make a decision; to provide some clarity for the day; or to solve a problem, based on your experience, that would take a team member a week to resolve.

It's an ongoing stretch for all leaders – consciously creating space and stepping out, or stepping in to be supportive, to relieve the pressure from their teams or maintain morale.

Time on the balcony and time on the dance floor are not in competition and needn't be mutually exclusive. Both can be helpful and productive places to be. What's needed is the judgement in how to divide your time to get the best of both. With limited hours in the day, there's a danger that leaders spread themselves too thinly. They try to do everything, be all things to all people and therefore don't make great decisions about when to step out onto the balcony.

As we will examine in the next chapter, this dilemma is far from insurmountable, and we'll talk about the steps you can take up to your balcony view.

First let's look at what we can learn from Charles Darwin, the nineteenth-century English naturalist, geologist and biologist, admired by many as one of the most influential figures in human history for his advances in modern evolutionary theory. Darwin had his own 'thinking path' at his Down House residence in Kent, England.

The path was a purposely constructed sand-covered walkway that still to this day winds through a wooded and hedge-lined trail that starts at and returns to the house. He would walk there twice each day, morning and afternoon. He is reported as often lining up a certain number of pebbles at the entrance to the path and kicking one away on each lap he completed. Sometimes his time on the thinking path would require the space for a three- or four-pebble problem.[29]

It's when people arrive on the balcony or the thinking path that we find our third tension emerging.

---

29 D Young, 'Charles Darwin's daily walks: The mental rewards of exercise' (*Psychology Today*, 12 January 2015), www.psychologytoday. com/intl/blog/how-to-think-about-exercise/201501/charles-darwins-daily-walks, accessed 30 October 2024

Tension 3: What to think about

Now I'm up here on the balcony and can see for miles, where do I start?

When you legitimise thinking time as a leadership activity, you commit yourself to explicit work. If you're accustomed to being knee-deep in the busyness of the day to day, a conscious effort is required to reorientate yourself to a different way of being *and* doing. You also need to make a deliberate shift in mindset, from viewing thinking time as some sort of mystical activity, to recognising thinking time as a powerhouse of innovation and productivity in an engine room of ideas.

Our experience of thinking time often comes from formalised and cooperative settings, for example, the retreat or the away day. You may be familiar with spacious rooms, an enticing coffee and pastries selection, responding to a set agenda, rich conversations with colleagues, an abundance of colourful Post-it notes and a wall full of flip charts. Here you develop ideas as a team, appreciate alternative points of view and debate respectfully. You might also be accustomed to working with a coach, whose role is to help you think, using well-honed questions and attentive listening to enable you to reflect, imagine, analyse, take action.

Environments like this are designed to be stimulating, productive, safe and focused. Interestingly, participants often tell us that they're just as tired after an away day or an appointment with their coach as they are after a typical day working flat out at their usual relentless pace.

'Aha!' we say sagely. 'That's because thinking *is* work.'

Your personal thinking time may well feel different. It may consist of you being in a familiar spot, at home or in the office, perhaps out for a walk with nothing to write on, or in a coffee shop watching the world go by with all its distractions.

You may be solitary, having activated your out-of-office autoresponder that lets your team know you're away for the morning. Time to yourself might suit you, or you may miss the energy you enjoy from interactions with others.

There may be front-of-mind questions that you want to pay attention to. Perhaps you find it easier to concentrate on a concrete problem to see if you can carve out a solution. Alternatively, you might be inclined to start with a blank sheet of paper and to see what happens.

There is no right or wrong way to go about thinking time. That can be half the trouble, though. Clients we work with raise perfectly reasonable questions, including:

- What do I need to think about?

- What's the process, if there is one?

- Where do I begin?

- What's the best environment to think in?

- Who do I do my thinking with?

- How do I protect my thinking time from the demands of the day?

Questions like this illustrate how much the prospect of thinking time can prompt hesitation, even for competent and confident leaders. As we know, our brains are not keen on the unfamiliar. There are instant physiological rewards to be had from following existing or repetitive patterns rather than moving towards uncertainty. Even with the best of intentions to commit ourselves to thinking time with a clear diary – whether in the quiet office, the open air or a café – there's still a danger we'll open our laptops, check our emails, dive into instant messenger conversations, reach for our phones and scroll our social media sites, or work through an established to-do list.

The tensions we've described above are ever present and real in the minds of anyone that's struggling to be the best leader they can. As one of our clients courageously shared when challenged with creating time to focus on strategy:

'My brain feels like mush when it comes to the long game. I can handle today's problems, but figuring out the next six months... it is just too much.'

These three tensions are felt by many leaders and contribute to the neglect of thinking time. In our next chapter we propose some practical steps to help correct the neglect and bring thinking time back onto the leadership agenda.

4

How To Stop Neglecting Your Thinking Time

As we turn our attention to how to stop the neglect of thinking time, let's revisit *Moon Safari*. The opening track, 'Femme d'Argent', is a contemplative instrumental that, on first listen, is unexpected in its pace and tonality. It was designed to encourage the listener to engage with the album in a different way rather than heading straight into the big-hitting lead single that propelled the band to international fame. Nicolas Godin of Air said, '"La femme d'Argent" could only be at the beginning or the end of the record… except that it was too good of a track to be last, and so it was first. But I did need to fight for it… a lot of people wanted to put "Sexy Boy" first.'[30]

---

30 A Bourgougnon, 'Nicolas Godin from AIR on the gear used in "Moon Safari"' (Reverb, 6 March 2018), https://reverb.com/uk/news/nicolas-godin-from-air-on-the-gear-used-in-moon-safari, accessed 30 October 2024

For us one of the compelling aspects of the *Moon Safari* story comes from the moments when Nicolas Godin and Jean-Benoît Dunckel both resist the swell of mainstream opinion, be that the musical trends of the era or their record company's preferences. The musicians stepped back, stopped what they were doing and made time to think instead of making knee-jerk decisions in the moment. Their approach defined their overall process from the beginning and they took the time to do what they knew was right for their vision. Their aim was to create something remarkable that would differentiate them from their peers.

As with the determined French duo, the move to make more time to think needs to come from you first. As we observed in our introduction, any leader who operates with the hopeful notion that at some point there will be a time to pause and think has a problem, because in reality, *that's never going to happen.*

The harsh truth is that there will be no future moment when the smoke clears and the fires are out. There will be no perfect set of conditions where you have time to sit back and think. Unless you make changes, your schedule will only become busier, other people's expectations of you will be more intense, and as a result, your capacity to work out what is really important will become even more blurred.

Twenty-first-century leadership literature illustrates this trap. Oliver Burkeman's philosophy, set out in his book *Four Thousand Weeks*, challenges received wisdom on productivity and the misconceived idea that we can make it to the end of our to-do list.[31] He explained that, even in our world full of demands and distractions, most advice on improving productivity only serves to make things harder for us. He says we are told we will one day get on top of all our tasks and learn to master our time, but even striving for that makes us busier, more distracted and more isolated. Meanwhile, we keep putting off the most important aspects of our lives, hoping in vain for the perfect time to focus on them.

Greg McKeown, in his book *Essentialism*, advocates for escaping the implausible ambition of doing everything. Instead he urges us to pursue 'the right thing, in the right way, at the right time'. He describes the approach as being: 'about regaining control of our own choices about where to spend our time and energies instead of giving others implicit permission to choose for us'.[32]

The action you need to take

The clear message is: if you want to exercise choice, discretion and judgement on where your time is spent

31 O Burkeman, *Four Thousand Weeks: Time management for mortals* (Vintage, April 2022)
32 G McKeown, *Essentialism: The disciplined pursuit of less* (Virgin Books, January 2021)

rather than allowing yourself to be limited, then it's time to act.

The first step is simple. Open your diary and take a look.

First action: Take back control of your diary

What's the story you see when you look at your diary? Packed? Overloaded?

If your time is not *your time* anymore, and if everyone simultaneously makes claims on your time, then – as pleasing as it might be for your ego to be in such demand – the fact is that you've lost control.

What are the options here? You can't buy yourself even one additional hour. Who can? Pick your millionaire: Kim Kardashian has impressive spending habits, but even she can't purchase more time.

It's time for a radical decision: to switch from serving your diary to your diary serving you. It may sound counterintuitive or potentially selfish (of which more later). However, we propose that making space to think about your team, boss, organisation, shareholders and stakeholders is the best way to deliver for them.

We challenge you to look at your diary for the next three months and take back three hours to give yourself time to think. There are two questions that can lead to a sensible place to start:

1. What can I stop doing?
2. What could others be doing instead of me?

How does the prospect of answering these questions make you feel? Frustrated? Excited? Helpless? Determined?

We invite you to sit with any of those feelings and continue to think about the questions. Do you sense a magnetic pull towards easy distractions? An example might be responding to outstanding invites, adding details to notes or reports, or noting a white paper you need to read before a meeting and adding it to your to-do list.

That's the *anxiety–distraction feedback loop*. Ignore it if you can, and come back to the questions.

Let's take them one by one:

1. What can I stop doing?

Let's start with a story.

CASE STUDY: Productive delegation

We were impressed when the senior executive for a large retailer came to speak to a cohort of leaders that we were working with. He had a great reputation in the organisation, having just completed a successful high-impact change (almost impossible to do, in our experience).

One of our questions was: 'How do you fit it all in?'

His response: 'I look in my diary and review all the meetings I'm invited to, and the first question I ask is: *Which of these meetings is a development opportunity for one of my team?* When I've worked that out, my team members go to the meetings and learn, and I save myself significant amounts of time.'

There's so much to admire in this approach:

- The lack of ego in liberating yourself from the belief that you're essential to every interaction

- Trust in your team

- Foresight to see meetings not as a chore for you but as a beneficial stretch for others

- Time created to spend on the work to which you can make the best contribution

Which of the meetings in your diary could represent great development for your team members if they deputised for you? Granted, you may need to allocate some preparation time with them ahead of the meeting itself. If so, we would see that as an investment that delivers pretty fast returns.

Let's stay on the subject of meetings you may not need to go to. Where are the others? They might be those that land in your diary without explanation or rationale. It may be the routine meetings whose usefulness is long out of date, where you never contribute, learn very little and wonder why you're there. It could be your weekly team meeting that you pride yourself on attending when – maybe, just maybe – your team might really enjoy having some working space without you.

What boundaries or rules do you have in your diary? For example, think about how your energy is at 8am. Perhaps that's one of your golden times of the day when you're at your clearest, most daring and most articulate; or perhaps you can't quite form a sentence that early and wish everyone would give you a bit of peace. Is your energy cycle in tune with your most important meetings? What could you do to recalibrate your current arrangements so that your meetings stimulate your thinking rather than drain your brain?

A successful practice we've noticed in some of our client organisations is breaking the back-to-back cycle by shortening meetings. Not radically – perhaps fifty minutes rather than an hour, or twenty minutes rather than thirty. Shorter meetings focus attention and give you an all-important break to breathe, think, step away from your screen or simply – anarchic as it sounds – do nothing for a bit. Ten minutes. It's a small and significant building block in taking back control of your diary.

One of our favourite writers, James Clear, in his book *Atomic Habits* (which we'll look at in more detail later), says that when setting out our ambitions for forming new habits, 'It is so easy to overestimate the importance of one defining moment and underestimate the value of making small improvements on a daily basis. Too often, we convince ourselves that massive success requires massive action.'[33]

2. What could others be doing instead of me?

We've talked about the potential of your team members deputising for you at meetings. What else might you be able to delegate?

When leaders use delegation as a task management system, two barriers emerge:

- Guilt at the prospect of handing over work to an already busy team

---

33   J Clear, *Atomic Habits: An easy & proven way to build good habits & break bad ones* (Avery, 2018)

- The calculation that doing any job yourself will make it faster, more accurate, *done properly, the way I like it*

When delegation is deployed as a development system, the emotional and practical perspectives change. We recommend thinking about what you have on your agenda that is important rather than urgent. If there's the pressure of a deadline, the sensible step is to delegate to your most trusted colleagues – those whose ability and outlook you have faith in. This type of delegation is pragmatic but it doesn't change anything.

When you take a longer view of what you're responsible for, it becomes possible to delegate to a wider range of people:

- Who do I believe is ready for a fresh challenge?

- Who has said they're ready for more responsibility?

- Whose potential am I not sure about yet, where I'd love to see what they are capable of with time and support?

In meeting our 'saving three hours in three months challenge', think creatively about who might really flourish if they had the opportunities you could offer them. Not to mention the space that could create for you.

As well as making time to think, taking back control of your diary has wider benefits:

- You can deepen trust with your colleagues when you demonstrate your belief in what they can do.
- Your team becomes more resilient because there's no single point of failure if you're not there.
- You foster a spirit of collaboration.
- Individuals feel more purposeful and involved.
- Your boss is impressed because you're not rattling from one reaction to the next.
- Your brain thanks you as the best of its functionality starts to open up.

Taking back control of your diary – carving out and protecting thinking time – is like buying or downloading the lead single. It's a first step, and an instant introduction to an artist and their work. Acting on your thinking time is closer to exploring a whole album – its layers, its richness, the overlooked tracks and surprises that make up the whole picture.

Second action: Start thinking

If only it was as easy as pressing play.

It's not unusual for leaders to tell us that, once they do tear themselves away from the noise and hubbub of the dance floor and head up to the balcony, they're not entirely sure what to do when they're up there. They're back to that opaque statement, *be more strategic.* The question is no longer *When?* – it's *How?*

Our Thinking Directions, illustrated in the figure below, offer you some practical help. We have identified four thinking direction categories, which you can choose from, based on your strategic challenges, your personal preferences or simply where your curiosity leads you.

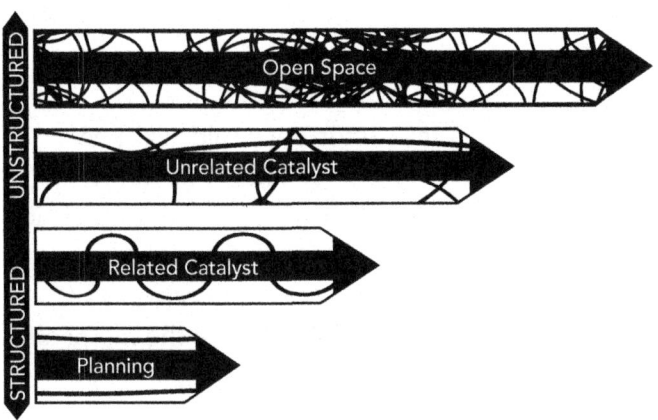

Thinking Directions

Each category offers a specific starting place and a direction to head in. We also include a set of open questions with each, as we know from our work with neuroscientists and leaders that inquiry stimulates powerful thinking zones of the brain. Your cortex can't resist a great question and fires up even if – in fact, *especially* if – you don't yet know the answer

Let's explore the four categories.

1. Open space

Open space means you start with only yourself, which will be anywhere between terrifying and exhilarating, depending on your personality type and your habits and practice. If you're at the terrifying end of the scale, we encourage you to persevere through the initial discomfort.

As a wise Pilates instructor once told us: 'Recognise the difference between pain and discomfort. If it's pain, stop. If it's only discomfort, work though it – you'll be far more flexible on the other side.'

If you're at the exhilarating end, enjoy the moment!

You might want to:

- **Clear your workspace to declutter your mind.**
  A clean environment can help reduce distractions and promote focus.

- **Shut down your laptop and head outside.**
  Disconnecting from digital devices and taking a walk outdoors can be incredibly refreshing. It

allows you to clear your mind, breathe in fresh air and gain new perspectives.

- **Change your environment.** Sometimes a shift of scenery can spark creativity. This could involve moving to a new room, going to a café or even just sitting in a different spot in the same room.

- **Set your phone to airplane mode.** Minimising distractions will help you stay with uninterrupted thinking.

- **Keep a small notebook handy.** This allows you to jot down ideas or thoughts as they come to you, regardless of where you are, and ensures you don't forget potentially valuable insights.

Notice where your thoughts go, and follow them for a while. Trust your instincts, suspend judgement on what is emerging, just let the thoughts flow. Make notes, draw diagrams or sketch pictures if that helps. Whether through active engagement or quiet reflection, finding what works best for you can greatly enhance your ability to generate new ideas and solutions.

This style of thinking probably benefits from having a time limit – perhaps twenty minutes to start with, moving to thirty minutes and then an hour as the space starts to be more familiar.

Once you reach your set time, reflect on what happened:

- Where did you go?

- What emerged most clearly (if anything)?

- What immediate insight can you draw from the experience?

- Which half-formed ideas do you want to keep and develop later?

- What do you feel energised to do immediately?

Capture any treasure in a form that you can return to.

2. Unrelated catalyst

Loved by creativity gurus, the *unrelated catalyst* direction begins with a stimulus not directly related to your role or your work environment. It might be a story, podcast, documentary, film, music, visual art, sporting moment, object or inspirational figure. You choose. Given how comfortable the brain becomes with repeated patterns, we advise you pick something that is new and unusual for you.

Invest some time in immersing yourself in your selected catalyst. Listen, look, observe and stay present. Be aware of your reactions, but don't do anything with them yet – your brain will remember. Then, having spent some time absorbed in your catalyst, come back to yourself.

Notice your immediate thoughts and follow any that are compelling:

- What connections come to you?

- What ideas, insights or inspirations?

- How might this catalyst help you break out of your usual assumptions and approaches and innovate?

Now turn to application:

- Where might any of this be helpful to you?

- What is possible in practical terms?

- What do you want to select to give more detailed attention to?

3. Related catalyst

The *related catalyst* starts with a specific provocation (if you like a more structured style of thinking, rejoice!).

We would love to have been at a post-pandemic leadership forum, for sixty leaders from a property development company, together with a commercial landlord, all of whom spent a whole day thinking about a single question: *What is the future of office space?*

Usually, the related catalyst appears in the form of a question. We also find that a problem statement, a new market development, an untested opportunity or a polarity (for example, *How do we deliver centralised quality standards and local market customisation?*) can act as great related catalysts.

The principles are:

- Choose an area that is directly related to your area of accountability, or that's relevant now and will be relevant in the future to the organisation you work with.

- Frame the issue as openly and constructively as possible so that you don't bias or limit your responses at an early stage.

- Identify open-ended questions that help you to catalyse your thinking. For example, *What do you need to do to be ready for [your challenge or opportunity]?* rather than *Are we prepared to face the risk of [your challenge or opportunity]?*

As your thoughts start to flow:

- Generate volume first – don't disregard or evaluate anything too early.

- Build one idea from another, or even use the opposite perspective to stimulate alternatives.

As with the open space direction, it can be helpful to set a time limit for this initial response.

The temptation is then to move to selection or prioritisation of ideas. Press pause there and instead look for *connections* – what you might synthesise with to create something new. Remember, *Moon Safari* came from the blending of multiple inputs and influences, not from a single template.

Once you have spotted the connections, choose the one or two options that you can take some early action on. Then identify what the starting point looks like, not just what the whole solution might be.

4. Planning

Strategic priorities, achieving your growth agenda, restructuring your team to reflect new ways of working, breaking down the impact of a legal or regulatory change that will come into force in the next twelve months, new projects on the horizon – these are all examples of work that sits easily in our important-but-not-yet-urgent column.

The *planning* direction is an opportunity to commit time to leading in the near, visible future. As you are doing so from a balcony view, you have several advantages:

• The opportunity to take a long, broad overview of what's involved

- Increased choice as to how you approach the scope and scale of what you need to do

- The ability to distinguish what is really significant

- Time to build trust with your stakeholders

- Options in terms of who you might delegate aspects of the work to as a development track for them

There are some well-established tools to offer structure and challenge in this direction of thinking:

- **Outcomes:** What you want to achieve

- **Purpose:** Why you want to achieve it

- **Milestones:** What you are going to do by when

- **Roles:** Who should do what and why

In our coaching work we find it staggering how powerful it is for our clients to simply make sense of basic administration and immediate schedules (in the next week or fortnight), clearing space and reprioritising.

With time for planning, you can also go beyond the obvious, consider different scenarios and work out your risk appetite rather than having to grapple with every decision from scratch.

Whether this involves top-level or detailed day-to-day diary management, this direction of thinking pays back immediately with a material output you can build on.

We hope that our four directions take away some of the mystery but none of the curiosity about thinking time. You may be delighted and relieved to hear that any of the directions will benefit from one or more people working with you. As Aristotle suggested, we are all more intelligent with someone on the receiving end of our thoughts. Consider who your thinking partners might be, and invite them to join you on the adventure.

Here's a reality check: you might already be telling yourself that you agree wholeheartedly with what we've said in this chapter and that, yes, you'll definitely set some time aside at the end of the month. Or maybe at the end of the quarter. Or perhaps at the very least at the end of your current project, possibly when your new deputy is appointed.

Except we all know that won't happen.

Face it. That perfect time is never coming. You might easily convince yourself to the contrary, but the reality is that the best time is now.

In fact, we'd suggest that having read this section, you step away from this book.

Just stop.

It's an easy decision.

Do nothing but think.

Even if only for a minute or two.

And take it all in.

Four short reflections from Caroline on making time to think

These are not overly profound or particularly new, but as we've heard so far, neglected acts rarely are.

1. 'I can't think without a pen in my hand'

Those who know me well will have heard me say this many a time: it's impossible for me to think expansively or clear my head while staring at a screen. I can get stuff done, but the thinking to activate that action is better done elsewhere, in a different space. I might doodle for a while or I might stare into the distance, both of which are just fine.

A pen, an open journal or a pack of Post-its and different space form my catalyst. The task is to empty my head – simple.

2. Mabel and I

I was a daily London commuter for many years, and the opportunity that provided for thinking was invaluable. The morning quiet and warmth of the train created a perfect environment to sit back and ponder. Thoughts would pop into my head, which I sometimes captured, while sometimes just letting them flow in then out was enough. That time on the train was 'the space in between', where nothing else needed to be done other than being still.

On my working-from-home days, recreating that morning thinking space has become critical to my wellbeing. My 'commute' is now with my dog, Mabel – fresher air, for sure!

3. Beware the action collector

I've been in several meetings recently where there is an increasing need to generate actions. It's almost as though the success of a meeting is determined by the length of the action list at the end, and progress is measured by obsessively tracking and ticking off these actions. There is often a lack of specificity in the action and little care given to the quality of any action, even if it is completed. I find this a superficial and frenetic way to work, and I have no doubt it leads to duplication and general inefficiency.

Of course, there are times when specific actions are required – urgent or otherwise – but I also firmly believe that if the right conversations are happening, the action will take care of itself.

What if you didn't leave a meeting with an action list, instead taking the time to reach a common understanding, or unblocking an issue that had been circling unanswered for some time? What if you actioned something important in the moment rather than taking it offline? Wouldn't that be a good use of collaborative thinking time?

4. Get out of your head

A few years ago, I found myself in a hectic phase of life. I was pulled in multiple directions, lurching from one thing to another: work deadlines, a young family, ageing parents, house renovations, social commitments and obligations. No time for self but also no time to think how to make things different.

I was drawn back to *somatic practice* to unlock this issue. Working in a supportive supervision group, with shared experience and belief in the power of somatic work, the wonderful Eunice Aquilina, an expert coach in somatic methodology, guided me through an exercise. This was a real and physical enactment of the pulls on my time that were impacting my ability to think clearly.

After some preparatory work sharing context, members of the group played the roles of the various people in need of some of my time. In turn, they began speaking. Then they spoke all at once, getting louder, shouting at me, calling for my attention, using the same language and phrases that those close to me would use, their voices getting louder and louder, more urgent and demanding. It was an incredibly intense and uncomfortable experience, and we repeated it several times.

My practice through all this commotion was to remain centred and to breathe. This was practised over and over, under the same pressure, to increase my capacity to respond wisely and consciously from a calmer, more considered position. Less head thinking, more bodily wisdom.

PART TWO
THE NEGLECT OF BUILDING TRUST

5
The Story Of *Low*
By David Bowie

B efore making *Low,* David Bowie trusted very few people. He was living in Los Angeles, having reached a peak of commercial success with his album *Young Americans,* released in 1975. The album gave Bowie his first US number-one chart position with 'Fame'.

Although his record label was thrilled by the sales results, and his extensive touring had attracted audiences across the United States, Bowie was in danger. His addiction to cocaine led to serious bouts of paranoia and reclusive living. The crisis was such that each morning his loyal assistant, Coco Schwab – one of the few people Bowie trusted – would place a mirror under his nose to check he was still breathing before waking him, wherever he had fallen asleep.[34]

Bowie was existing in an extremely difficult personal place, both physically and mentally. He was tied into a restrictive financial contract with his previous manager, meaning he saw little of the fruits of his success. Bowie's first marriage was in crisis, he was disillusioned with the music industry, and he was at odds with his own creative journey. Fortunately, driven by a belief that he needed to find new ways of making music, he decided it was time to save his own life.

The new journey began at the Château d'Hérouville, near Paris. It included a trusted friend, Iggy Pop, and Brian Eno, together with a mix of other long-standing and new musical contributors. Although they had met backstage in 1976, Bowie and Eno had not yet worked together but, through their mutual admiration, had begun building a personal relationship. Eno's album, *Another Green World*, struck a chord with Bowie, who was caught by its subtle complexities of sounds and textures. The men were united in their ambition to experiment and to discover a 'new musical language'.

---

34   P Doggett, *The Man Who Sold the World: David Bowie and the 1970s* (Vintage, 2012)

While the music and lyrics of what eventually became *Low* convey dislocation, unease, loneliness and yearning, the connection between the people who made it was developing in a different way.

While living at the château, Bowie, Eno and Iggy Pop, as well as the other musicians working with them, spent significant time together. It was a conscious decision on David Bowie's part to live and socialise with his fellow collaborators throughout and build shared experiences, as opposed to retiring to his own isolation at the end of the working day. They ate together every night, told each other stories and watched *Fawlty Towers*, which became a shared reference in terms of humour. By the time they relocated to Cold War Berlin to complete their work, they were already a tight-knit group. They had laid the foundations for high trust.

The bond of trust between Bowie and his band was so secure, together they felt safe and strong enough to take on the risks that lay ahead. The team was completed with the arrival of producer Tony Visconti, new to the project but a long-standing Bowie collaborator.

As they arrived to work at the relatively cheap Hansa Studios, next to the Berlin Wall in the American sector, Bowie and his troupe were pretty much unknown in the city. In West Berlin's liberal and easygoing atmosphere they could hang out in discotheques, bars and cafés and walk the streets without being recognised.

Once work began on *Low*, no ideas were off limits. Fresh concepts were instead given free rein to roam, to be nurtured and to flourish. When Visconti's four-year-old son was heard playing around on the piano, even that motif was included.

The musicians chopped and changed instruments, pushing beyond the familiar to expand their artistic horizons. The *Low* team played with the acoustics at Hansa Studios, with the unconventional possibilities of synthesisers (not just reproduced brass or string sections but, as Bowie said, 'the mistakes that they made, that we found more interesting than the stuff they were supposed to do'), and with Brian Eno's Oblique Strategies cards.[35]

An active part of the process had been creating, early on, a set of relationships based on trust. Each member contributing to the music made in Paris and Berlin was invested in it.

Everybody felt able to bring fresh thinking to the table, irrespective of how outlandish and unconventional the ideas may have sounded. Today we might describe what they created as *psychological safety*.

Bowie himself reflected on this in a 2002 interview:

---

35   E Deane and H Thompson, *Rock & Roll* (WGBH Educational Foundation, 1995)

'I believe that I often bring out the best in somebody's talents. To not be modest about it, you'll find that with only a couple of exceptions, most of the musicians that I've worked with have done their best work by far with me.'[36]

After *Low* was completed, Bowie was uncertain that anybody would ever hear it. His record company, RCA, actively considered not releasing it, believing the album represented commercial disaster – its eleven tracks subverted conventional song structures, and the B-side consisted of four purely instrumental tracks (apart from a few lines in an improvised language on 'Warszawa').

Tony Visconti summed up how the team felt about the risks of the album not seeing the light of day: 'Well, I don't care because a month spent in the studio with Bowie and Eno is never a waste of my life.'[37]

In fact, *Low* was a commercial success, peaking at number two on the UK Albums Chart and number eleven on the US Billboard Top LPs and Tape chart. The lead single, 'Sound and Vision', was used as background

---

36   'Interview with David Bowie' (*ConcertLivewire.com*, 16 June 2002), www.concertlivewire.com/interviews/bowie.htm, accessed 31 October 2024

37   W Hermes, 'How David Bowie, Brian Eno revolutionized rock on "Low"' (*Rolling Stone*, 13 January 2017), www.rollingstone.com/music/music-features/how-david-bowie-brian-eno-revolutionized-rock-on-low-117033, accessed 31 October 2024

music for BBC continuity announcements at the time, enhancing its profile even further.

Low was profoundly influential in the years to come and is now regarded as a hugely significant album – brave, original and ahead of its time.

What we can learn from David Bowie about building trust

There are three main areas around trust that can be learned from David Bowie:

1. **The power of taking time to build mutual trust with your team and collaborators.** *Fawlty Towers* might not magically bond teams together in the twenty-first century, but shared time, shared meals and shared experiences are potent, and the return on investment is palpable.

2. **The impact of being open to the different styles, skills and abilities other people can bring to fulfil your vision.** This is illustrated by the approach employed by Iggy Pop, Brian Eno, Tony Visconti and the other *Low* musicians. Trust allows people a safe space in which to stretch themselves, see the value of their contribution and innovate, with all the excitement, empowerment and engagement this generates. Performance levels accelerate. People are prepared to take risks.

3. **The importance of facing the truth together with your collaborators.** It is much easier to fulfil your own potential with people around you that you genuinely trust and who are unafraid to tell you the truth, as Bowie's assistant Coco consistently did.

We invite you to take a moment of reflection and ask yourself whether there is enough trust in your relationships, your teams and your organisation. When trust does flourish, the extraordinary becomes possible, opening space for growth, success and personal fulfilment.

We instinctively know this, so why has trust become a neglected act of leadership?

We will explore this question in our next chapters.

6

Why We Neglect Building Trust

In this chapter we examine why we believe that building trust is a neglected act of leadership. We also aim to shed light on the perfect storm of global, organisational and personal phenomena that means trust is no longer assured if we don't take action to build it.

As we do so, we invite you to have some questions in mind:

- What does it take for you to trust a colleague, boss or direct report?

- How much time do you devote to thinking about what will encourage them to place their trust in you?

- When you review a typical month in your diary, how many actions are there that are directly or indirectly about building trust?

We'll start with a story about a CEO that illustrates how a lack of trust can develop, even when a leader deliberately demonstrates his confidence in his team, with the intention of *increasing* trust.

CASE STUDY: Unintended neglect

We worked recently with the CEO (of a tech company) – we'll call him John – who prided himself on being approachable, operating an open-door policy and having a warm and informal style in meetings. It was only when his new HR director questioned employee engagement that a note of self-doubt crept in.

This prompted the realisation that there was a gap between intention and practice. One-to-one time with John's team had been relegated to quarterly reviews and emergencies. Lost in product launches and growth, he hadn't noticed the growing disconnect between himself and the people who reported into him.

Determined to fix things, John booked a series of individual conversations with his team, starting with the lead developer, a quiet genius who produced impeccable work. Diving in with a prepared speech about open communication, John was surprised by the awkward silence that followed.

'Honestly,' the developer finally mumbled, 'we mostly just need clear direction. Knowing you see the bigger picture keeps us motivated.'

The following day, in a similar sit-down, John met with the head of finance, who confessed anxieties about keeping up with the company's rapid growth. This director had never voiced their concerns because they didn't want to seem incompetent. Even the extraverted head of operations admitted feeling invisible most days.

By the end of the week, John looked at himself in the mirror, coming to terms with the version of himself seen by his team and understanding the consequences of his unintended neglect. He now understood the HR director's concern.

John had a team of talented, passionate people who were asking for more than quick instructions and deadlines. Individuals in the team needed to be seen, to be heard, to feel like a part of something bigger than themselves. Despite the CEO's best intentions, these significant relationships had been maintained at arm's length. This hadn't been a deliberate choice, but it had become the status quo that nobody felt able to question.

The result was an absence of trust – with risks to relationships, honesty, motivation and performance – until the situation was actively addressed.

In much of our work, helping individuals and teams to cultivate trust and engagement is integral. It's rare to encounter someone who doesn't aspire to great working relationships, and we routinely witness the performance boost, healthier culture and improved wellbeing that comes with paying attention to trust.

Conversely, we've observed the consequences when leaders and organisations fall into a habit of neglect. Those consequences include:

- Less effective meetings
- Increased perception of political agendas
- Decisions becoming stuck
- Blockages in communication and collaboration
- Higher stress for individuals

There's a persuasive and well-established body of research indicating that organisations characterised by high trust – and therefore healthy engagement, psychological safety, talent retention and risk appetite – are the ones that succeed, endure and compete.

Examples of this include Gallup's research highlighting the positive impact of high employee engagement, including lower turnover, improved productivity and profitability.[38]

In 2023 *MIT Sloan Management Review* published an article on high-trust workplaces, including research calculating that: 'Trusting employees are 260% more

---

38   T Nolan et al., 'The benefits of employee engagement' (Gallup, 20 June 2013), www.gallup.com/workplace/236927/employee-engagement-drives-growth.aspx, accessed 31 October 2024

motivated to work, have 41% lower rates of absentee-ism, and are 50% less likely to look for another job.'[39]

However, the same article added a significant finding: 'We also found that roughly 1 in 4 workers don't trust their employer.'

Mercer's 2024 'Global Talent Trends' report found a declining picture of organisational trust. Their research reveals that the trust that employers will do the right thing for employees has declined from 80% in 2022 to 69% in 2024.[40]

The assumption leaders may have made – that trust should reflect one's own character, ability and authenticity – is no longer enough in environments where there is a growing inclination to question authority, directives and decisions.

---

39 A Reichheld and A Dunlop, 'How to build a high-trust workplace: The more your employees trust you, the more engaged they'll be' (*MIT Sloan Management Review*, 24 January 2023), https://sloanreview.mit.edu/article/how-to-build-a-high-trust-workplace, accessed 31 October 2024

40 Mercer, *Workforce 2.0: Unlocking human potential in a machine-augmented world* (Mercer Talent Trends, 2024), www.mercer.com/assets/global/en/shared-assets/local/attachments/pdf-2024-global-talent-trends-report-en.pdf, accessed 31 October 2024

The global perspective

Elvis Presley's hips and *Heartbreak Hotel* in the 1950s. Flowers in your hair and Woodstock in the 1960s. Johnny Rotten's sneer and the riotous emergence of punk in the 1970s. Smiley faces on the way to raves in fields in the 1980s. Thumbing through *No Logo* by Naomi Klein at the end of the 1990s.

Choose your preferred twentieth-century cultural moment, but whichever one resonates most with you, each has contributed to the position you find yourself in as a leader in the twenty-first century, unable to take trust in your authority or even your integrity for granted.

The decline of trust in authority

The societal shifts we've witnessed in workplaces in the West are described by Robin Ryde, in his book *Never Mind the Bosses*, as 'the death of deference'.[41] The automatic, polite esteem and respect – based on power, status, age or experience – that may have been assured have now been eroded. The hippie movement rejected the values and lifestyle of previous generations – the despised 'straights'. The punk generation then adopted a DIY ethos that no longer relied on the establishment or big business to realise its ambitions.

---

41 R Ryde, *Never Mind the Bosses: Hastening the death of deference for business success* (Jossey-Bass, 2012)

Record labels and magazines were set up in kitchens not corporates; clothes were bought from charity shops not high street chains, and then ripped up and reinvented.

We've reached a point where society's traditional pillars have shaky foundations, and this is not just because of successive youthquakes. Once admired businesses have been undermined by their own behaviour, from supply chain irregularities to the use of cheap and exploited labour, and by irresponsible environmental disasters through to successive financial crises.

Respect for one's bank manager dissipated when it emerged that banks had mis-sold spurious financial products to customers rather than keeping their money safe and their savings secure. Today, with banks disappearing from the high street into call centres and onto apps, and more recently introducing chatbots to provide customer service, relationships with clients are more remote. As a result, financial institutions no longer enjoy the trust they used to.

Similarly, organisations whose authority was once unquestioned find themselves in much less comfortable positions today. Not for the first time, the Metropolitan Police in the UK have suffered severe reputational damage after criminal activities, including sexual assault, rape and murder by serving officers. Both the Roman Catholic Church and Church of England have also been exposed and held accountable for abuses of power, including the sexual exploitation of children.

Add to this dismal list the revelations in the film and television industries – at the highest level – when claims of sexual harassment and intimidation by those who held power and influence over people and their careers became public knowledge thanks to social media activism and investigative journalism. Journalists themselves, previously admired as seekers of truth, have fared little better in reputational terms, facing questions and enquiries into how they acquire exclusive stories, along with the proliferation of digital media sources operating with varied standards of reliability and the aroma of 'fake news'.

If the second half of the twentieth century represents the slow decline of trust in authority, the twenty-first century – when the counterculture moved online – had extraordinary consequences for who we choose to trust. We are spoilt for choice.

Published lives

The scale and style of social media platforms is eye-watering. At time of writing, the active monthly users of Facebook, YouTube, TikTok, LinkedIn, X (formerly known as Twitter) and Reddit run into millions or billions per platform. This means that the details of our personal lives, and the representations of who we are, what we do and what we think can be selected, edited and shared widely to people we have never met.

This apparently intimate information leads to the phenomenon of parasocial relationships, ie, one-sided psychological attachment to politicians, business figures, actors, influencers and other celebrities. We find ourselves caring passionately about what they do and say and what is said about them. While the emotions experienced in the heat of parasocial relationships are real, the relationships themselves are based on illusion. However, the reality is that our sense of who people are is drawn from highly curated versions of their experiences, preferences and personal traits, on the basis that no authentic work has been done to build trust, rapport and understanding, despite the time we might spend scrolling timelines and immersing ourselves in content published by others (or by their professional PR and content creators).

Instead, our alternatives for interaction are reaction buttons and comments sections. Entrepreneurs who use personalised profiles to promote themselves on social media platforms have acknowledged that the comments they receive can be an invaluable source of feedback. This raises an intriguing thought for leaders: what if every meeting you chaired or presentation you gave was subject to likes or sad-face – and worse – emojis and to anonymised views on how you did? We would argue that this is a day-to-day reality rather than a *What if?* We are subject to, for example, reviews on the quality of leadership at individual organisations on Glassdoor, or the private-chat function on virtual meeting platforms, or the team WhatsApp groups we're not part of.

Is this performance-enhancing, or terrifying? However it is for you, the idea that people may be judging you without your knowledge is hardly conducive to trust.

The prevalence of published lives brings with it mass access to commentary on others and the option to be anonymous when talking about them. If the online community decides not to trust someone based on shared information – whether that is verified or not – thousands worldwide can quickly share and spread that opinion without fact checking. Reputations can be instantly built or destroyed.

While you may not be managing a Cristiano Ronaldo- or Selena Gomez-scale Instagram profile, liquid expectations (the idea that customer expectations are fluid and extend beyond boundaries) might mean that your key stakeholders have an expectation of what they should know about you to trust you. They may also have formed the habit of making snap judgements, not always evidence-based, on whether you are trustworthy or not.

A generational shift in the perception of authority

One of our long-established financial services clients provides us with an example of how CEOs now have to work to build trust.

CASE STUDY: Breaking down barriers

The organisation has an annual intake of graduates, and its influential CEO liked to meet the new entrants early on in their programme, hosting a Q&A session in the CEO's grand and well-appointed office.

At one time this was a hushed and deferential event, where the limited number of questions would often be planted by the HR team. However, times and expectations have changed. Graduates no longer sit on their hands looking uncomfortable. They actively challenge the CEO on investment decisions or interrogate the organisation's culture and value systems.

The CEO said that they enjoyed this shift, since it made it a more lively and engaging experience for them too. However, even they were surprised when one graduate, as they were leaving, said, 'It's been great to meet you. Call me – we should do lunch.'

Legend has it that the CEO accepted the invitation, which is credible, given that organisation's strategy included a priority to connect with and appeal to a younger customer base.

The post-pandemic world

Before the Covid pandemic swept the world, how frequently did you use video conferencing platforms (Zoom, Teams, Skype, etc) for your regular meetings?

While some global and remote teams were familiar with the practice, suddenly in 2020 they became the dominant reality for many people. Scattered as we all were in our homes in widely different locations, the use of these platforms had interesting impacts on relationships:

- We lost physical, spontaneous contact with those we were most closely connected to in the daily workplace.

- We gained new glimpses into colleagues' lives – their home space, pets, children and partners became part of the mix – leading to a sense of greater informality.

- It was simpler to connect with widely distributed groups of people, meaning new networks and conversations.

- For many leaders the belief that it was imperative to see their people all the time to understand or manage what they were doing was debunked.

- Leaders' assumptions were disrupted as they discovered people were highly productive while they worked, unsupervised, from home.

As remote working became standard, we found that the leaders who routinely checked in with their employees were the ones who thrived and weathered the crisis with more resilience. Rather than police their employees' work rate, they made space to share personal experiences or enquire about their wellbeing. As a result, they deepened trust with their teams.

This wasn't a universal experience. While productivity rose during the pandemic, so did burnout. Those who joined organisations during lockdowns found it much more difficult to make contacts, discover who they should or could be talking to, and absorb their new organisation's culture. As one of our clients said: 'How can we expect our new joiners to feel part of an organisation they only see through a screen on their kitchen table?'

The negotiation of post-pandemic working – whether direct, indirect, formal or informal – has been complex. Flexibility is prized to the point of being a deal breaker for some in deciding who they want to work for. Organisations' modi operandi have swung from exercising high discretion in working patterns to developing clear mandates about returning to the office. Both can be controversial, and it's difficult to make everyone happy or to enhance mutual trust.

Alongside flexible working, the potential of AI in the workplace has become a dominant topic. Once again, data reveals a mix of attitudes: Korn Ferry's

'Workforce 2024' report found that '65% of global workers under 55 are excited about the potential of AI' and that '70% of people who fear that AI will replace their job are now considering or actively looking for a new job.'[42]

Gallup's 2023 'State of the Global Workforce' report described the phenomenon of quiet quitting as 'what happens when someone psychologically disengages from work. They may be physically present or logged into their computer, but they don't know what to do or why it matters. They also don't have any supportive bonds with their coworkers, boss or their organization.'[43]

Gallup found that six out of ten of their respondents were in this category.

Perhaps what we're actually seeing, though, is a fundamental shift in our relationship with work. In 2024 *The New York Times* reported the viral spread of the hashtag *gross outfits at work* among young workers in China.[44] Those employees are choosing to wear 'intentionally lacklustre' outfits, sharing their looks

---

42 Korn Ferry, *Workforce 2024* (Korn Ferry, 2024), www.kornferry.com/content/dam/kornferry-v2/featured-topics/pdf/workforce-2024-report.pdf, accessed 31 October 2024

43 Gallup, *State of the Global Workplace: 2023 Report* (Gallup, 2024), www.gallup.com/workplace/349484/state-of-the-global-workplace.aspx, accessed 31 October 2024

44 C Fu and D Wakabayashi, 'Furry slippers and sweatpants: Young Chinese embrace "gross outfits" at work' (*The New York Times*, 31 March 2024), www.nytimes.com/2024/03/24/business/china-gross-outfits-at-work.html, accessed 31 October 2024

on social media platforms and competing to see whose casual, mismatched outfit is the most repulsive. The phenomenon has been described as 'responsible protest', demonstrating that younger workers arc attracted to the idea of 'lying flat', ie, opting for an easier, less effortful life rather than the dedication, striving and compliance with standards that characterised previous generations.

Where is trust in all of this? Wherever it is, it can no longer be taken for granted.

The organisational perspective

We have described a global picture in which trust no longer goes hand in hand with authority, relationships are more complex to navigate, and genuinely knowing who somebody is can feel elusive. Now we examine what is happening in organisational life.

New ways of working

The hybrid model – combining remote and in-person work – remains a work in progress for many organisations. As with any new practice in its early stages, we are still assessing what effective and less effective behaviour looks like.

As mentioned earlier in this chapter, enforced home working during the pandemic was a revelation to many managers, who discovered that their teams were productive and committed employees at home, despite the absence of constant supervision.

Questions about how to build trust in a hybrid world remain unresolved. Can lasting human connections be formed if we don't share social as well as working time? What replaces the spontaneous moments at the desk or in the coffee shop, in a world where everything is scheduled and diary space is rare?

In an online article, 'Are your team members lonely?', Constance N Hadley and Mark Mortenson revealed that 76% of executives they reviewed had difficulty making connections with their work team mates, and 58% described their work-based friendships as 'superficial'.[45] Add to this the fact that, since the turn of the century, job tenures have become shorter, making it more difficult to build relationships with colleagues before they move on.

The growth of zero-hour contracts has also contributed to a more transient workforce, whose psychological contract with their employers is different. The numbers illustrate the level of disruption over time:

- Millennials have a 34% shorter job tenure than any other generation in the workplace.

45 CN Hadley and M Mortenson, 'Are your team members lonely?' (*MIT Sloan Management Review*, 8 December 2020), https://sloanreview.mit.edu/article/are-your-team-members-lonely, accessed 31 October 2024

- Generation Z are 135% more likely to be in part-time or contract roles than millennials or baby boomers.

- In 2010, 0.4% of people worked on zero-hours contracts. By 2022, that increased to 3.4%.

LS:N, a trends intelligence and consumer foresight platform, shares an article entitled 'British Gen Z workers treat employers like bad dates'.[46] The article describes the trend known as *job ghosting*, where Gen Z job seekers abandon their new roles and new employers within a short time – sometimes even immediately after being hired – because they want to feel in charge of their careers.

Hybrid structures and changing patterns of employment are not the only factors in this mix. In a 2019 nationally representative study of over 14,000 US employees, Gallup found that 72% of employees were working on matrixed teams.[47]

Matrix structures have well-documented advantages, including:

- Greater autonomy for individuals

- Multidisciplinary teams

---

46 A Crossley et al., 'Stat: British Gen Z workers treat employers like bad dates' (LS:N Global, 21 February 2024), www.lsnglobal.com/article/view/30499, accessed 31 October 2024

47 R Sutton and B Wigert, 'Too many teams, too many bosses: Overcoming matrix madness' (Gallup, 19 October 2021), www.gallup.com/workplace/354935/teams-bosses-overcoming-matrix-madness.aspx, accessed 31 October 2024

- Skills development

- Effective use of resources

- Success in the delivery of complex projects

In a weak matrix structure, however, threats to trust emerge. Where there is lack of clarity on authority, priorities, responsibilities or decision making, impaired trust can arise.

A further risk in a dynamic matrix can be the very human dilemma of knowing exactly where people belong. One of our clients shared with us a question that came up when implementing a large matrixed project: 'Who will I have my Christmas lunch with?'

Who do we trust most now?

Michael Kuzminov, chief growth officer at HypeFactory, a global influencer marketing agency, noted in Forbes: 'Gen Z consumers are warier of trusting businesses compared to older generations and tend to place more trust in influencers that they deem to be authentic and relatable.'[48]

---

48 M Kuzminov, 'What should you know about Gen Z to drive your business?' (*Forbes*, 4 January 2023), www.forbes.com/sites/ forbesagencycouncil/2023/01/04/what-should-you-know-about-gen-z-to-drive-your-business, accessed 31 October 2024

At one time, leaders would have been confident that they and their organisations would be second on the list of whom to trust, behind family and friends. However, research shows that for Generation Z, at least, that has changed. An interloper has superseded the employer.

Social media networks now sit at position number two on Generation Z's trust barometer, with their employers and work colleagues trailing behind. Perhaps this shouldn't surprise us – not just because digital natives have grown up with technology as a defining feature of their life, but also because of the higher likelihood of this age group being in part-time or contract roles.

At a time when it is estimated that we have the highest number of generations in the total workforce, it's easy to focus on our differences. In fact, research carried out by Kronos (now UKG Workforce Institute) identified that Generation Z want very human things from their managers.[49] Specifically, that they:

- Trust them (47%)

- Support them (40%)

- Care about them (35%)

---

49 A Vegas, *Generation Z in the Workplace* (Kronos, 16 November 2019), www.scribd.com/document/581178509/3-gen-Z-Full-Report-Generation-Z-in-the-Workplace, accessed 31 October 2024

With the risk of less connectivity in our working lives and – as we discovered as we wrote this book – more data on what makes the different generations in the workplace distinctive, intriguing questions arise:

- Do we live in an ever increasingly polarised society?

- To what extent do you hold beliefs that are vastly different from those of the people you report to, or who report to you?

- To what extent do you feel it is possible to disagree agreeably?

This has an impact on some of the personal factors that could lie behind the neglect of building trust.

The personal perspective

After the powerful global and organisational perspectives, we need to pay particular attention to the personal perspective. Building trust on a personal level is more vital than ever.

Uncertainty about offence

In the West we are attuned to the notion that free speech is a basic human right, but even the most casual conversation in the workplace can bear more risk than ever before of becoming inflammatory. Politics, economics, the urgency of action on the environment, vaccines, gender, race, sexual orientation, rights and responsibilities, social and personal values – it seems there's no single consensus on any number of subjects as well as a sense that causing offence is ever more likely.

A Google Ngram (which collates how many times a word or phrase is used in bodies of published writing) sees a rapid increase in the phrase 'easily offended' from the year 2000 onwards. Frequency is at its highest level since 1830, when duels – rather than Twitter/X spats – might have been an option to resolve matters. The phrase was at its lowest frequency in the 1980s. The current workplace, with its multiple generations, includes people from the 1980s to today.

Movements including Black Lives Matter and #MeToo have amplified the complexity of some of the issues involved. Many organisations have responded with growing emphasis on inclusive leadership and interventions around diversity, equity, inclusion and unconscious bias. The extent to which this attention goes beyond superficial understanding and limited change is not yet clear.

Leaders thus find themselves operating in a highly sensitised environment, where they are also expected to be open and honest. *Authentic* and *vulnerable* may be the most overused words in conversations about leadership in recent times, but leaders are genuinely afraid of causing offence.

Leaders coached by The Oxford Group have also articulated their awareness that their own lived experiences don't match those of their workforce. This heightens their concern about saying anything that might appear to lack understanding or empathy. The temptation is to avoid the dilemma and stay silent, since it's easier not to have those interactions rather than figure out how to overcome personal discomfort.

There are significant consequences for trust here. If open conversations don't take place, we can only guess at what others believe and therefore their intentions and what their judgements are based on. To trust leaders, we need some level of faith in both their intentions and their judgement.

Where the intention to deepen understanding is clear, in most cases it is better to have the conversation than to avoid it, as illustrated in the following example.

CASE STUDY: Overcoming uncertainty

Andy experienced the need to deepen understanding when he was keen to start a conversation with a valued and highly respected team member. He procrastinated for some time, eventually realising that the fear of offence was holding him back.

Over time, Andy had noticed his colleague's hesitancy to join certain work-related social gatherings. He suspected this might be due to their religious beliefs.

He approached his colleague privately, expressing his appreciation for their contributions and role on the team. He shared his observation that his colleague tended not to take part in social activities, emphasising that this was entirely understandable and asking if it was possible to speak about solutions or options that were more appropriate for him.

This opened a dialogue in which the colleague shared deep insight into their faith and what this meant in a professional context. The conversation helped Andy to understand his colleague's belief, its importance, and the considerations that person needed to be true to himself while also functioning effectively as a member of the team. As a result, small changes were made, leading to more inclusive future agendas.

Unfortunately, these types of conversations between leaders and their team members feel like a rarity these days. Excess caution in taking on messier topics leads to missed opportunities to build understanding, empathy, mutual respect and mutual trust.

Chat, not conversation

We also need to examine the risk that we're becoming less practised at conversations as we become more frequent users of chat. Chat function technology has been available since the early 1970s and has grown gradually – and grew exponentially during the pandemic – for organisational, business and social users.

There are features in chat that make connectivity easier and more convenient. These include instant access, immediacy, several people in a conversation at once, and sharing pictures, links, documents and messages. Our growing use of chat is reinforced by the options that businesses offer to their customers. According to research attributed to JD Power, live chat is the preferred style of contact for customers with organisations, with 42% of customers preferring it compared to email (23%) and social media platforms (16%).[50] Based on this and other data, organisations are investing rapidly in the option of live chat for customers, meaning we reinforce our chat habits.

For human beings and human brains, however, instant access to people via chat limits the potential to build trusting relationships in which we feel safe. To achieve this, we need more profound connections, built on listening, and physical and mental engagement, that help us discover together and share insights.

---

50   S Macdonald, '25 reasons live chat can help you grow your business in 2023' (SuperOffice.com, 20 October 2022), www.superoffice. com/blog/live-chat-statistics/?utm_source=thejuice&utm_ medium=content-distribution&utm_campaign=thejuice-distribution, accessed 31 October 2024

How much is the risk of neglecting trust increased in a world in which the convenience of chat trumps the compassion of conversation?

In the face of this volatile, emotionally complex and at times bewildering set of circumstances, the arguments for and rewards of building trust are still persuasive and well worth striving for. There are clear and practical steps that leaders can take, although on the way, there are tensions to recognise and resolve. We examine those in the next chapter.

7
Building Trust: Three Tensions

Our belief is that the neglect of building trust is far from deliberate. Furthermore, our clients know trust matters. In this chapter we acknowledge and explore the dilemmas that make it difficult to prioritise building trust even though we know how vital it is.

The published evidence includes Google's Project Aristotle, which launched in 2012 and aimed to identify the factors that contribute to a team's performance and productivity. It studied Google's top-performing teams, collecting and analysing a wide range of data through surveys and interviews. The project identified *psychological safety* as the differentiating characteristic of their highest-performing teams.[51]

What prevents us building trust

We work with several organisations who have made high trust a wide-reaching organisational aspiration. The intention may be strong and well supported, but the reality is trickier. Once again, there are three over-riding tensions to acknowledge and resolve.

Tension 1: Pace versus space

How do I deliver everything that's expected of me and make time for other people?

A leader's typical day? Filled with back-to-back meetings, deadlines, targets, to-dos, to-don'ts. KPIs set, met or failed; prioritise this, not that; snap decision here, backburner there. Data, dashboards and budgets; forecasts to take in; agenda items to take out. Agree, disagree, negotiate, issue, cancel, order, hire and fire. You probably recognise this.

Leaders regularly tell us that they work beyond the pace that humans can normally cope with. By way

---

51   S Challinor, 'Project Aristotle: What Google uncovered about building successful teams' (Leaders of Great Britain, 4 June 2022), www. leadersgb.co.uk/news/project-aristotle-what-google-uncovered-about-building-successful-teams, accessed 31 October 2024

of consolation, surely nobody can ever accuse you of being neither important nor effective because you are always so busy? That's what leadership demands, isn't it – being all things to all people, the axis around which the business revolves? Also, because you are both dedicated and conscientious, these demands eat up every bit of space.

We've already considered how this pace destroys effective thinking time. As well as impeding on the space to reflect, this pace threatens the space to connect with others. When you barely have time to focus on yourself, where is the opportunity to take action to build trust with the people around you?

Stephen R Covey wrote, 'With people, fast is slow and slow is fast.'[52] Conscious engagement with your team members requires you to slow down and genuinely see them. The problem is, how do you quieten the mind while holding a million and one things in your head?

Two risks emerge unless we actively address this tension:

1. Trust-building interactions are deprioritised in the face of relentless activity, and we work on the optimistic assumption that everyone is OK until they say – or show – that they are not.

---

52   SR Covey, *7 Habits of Highly Effective People* (Simon & Schuster UK, May 2020)

2. The distractions of your packed diary prevent you from being fully present in the moment, so the quality of your conversations is diminished, even if you ever manage to make time for them.

There is a real danger that you stop seeing people as individuals and that one person blurs into another. You can't have a relationship with a haze of faces. Your responsibilities weigh heavily on you, impairing your capacity to properly assess people's capabilities, or how far they've developed in competence and confidence. You miss the cues that could tell you if they are content, indifferent or struggling.

To survive, you become more self-reliant than you need to be and fall into the default mindset of *It's easier if I do it myself*. Rather than demonstrating trust in your team by including them in problem solving, or delegating work to them that could offer development opportunities and renewed motivation, you become a remote figure taking action alone. As a result, your team has no clear sense of how you view them – or whether you care.

Having limited experience of each other at work doesn't stop our automatic brains (described by the Nobel Prize-winning psychologist Daniel Kahneman in Chapter 7 of his bestselling book as 'machines for jumping to conclusions'[53]) deciding who we think

---

53   D Kahneman, *Thinking, Fast and Slow* (Penguin, 2012)

people are. This is especially true for leaders whose behaviour is scrutinised, analysed and interpreted more intensively the more senior they become.

If you're not deliberately making space for active, trust-building conversations, then people have to decide whether to trust you, based on the flimsiest of evidence and without much human connection and meaningful engagement. It's a risk for everyone involved.

Tension 2: EQ to IQ (and back again)

How can I be both an emotionally intelligent colleague and have a brilliant analytical brain in the space of an hour?

Your morning: an unscheduled conversation with a team member about a personal and sensitive matter they're facing, followed without a break by an online meeting with your boss and peers to review team progress against targets. One conversation needs to be emotionally literate and empathic; while in the other your ability to pore over a spreadsheet, grasping the overall picture, its pertinent detail and insight, has to be crisp and clear.

The problem is that without the necessary time to decompress from one and to prepare for the other, you may find yourself with what could be described as *cognitive whiplash*. For the individual leader, the switch from one to the other and back again can be exhausting and disorientating. We know that versions of this pattern repeat themselves for our clients, day in and day out.

The presence of trust in this situation can reduce the jeopardy. Where we trust someone's intention and believe they usually do their best to see and hear us, we'll forgive a little distractibility on occasion. Equally, if we respect someone's judgement, we'll overlook some hesitation in assessing a complex calculation or potential risk, knowing that this is them on a bad day rather than a reflection of their overall competence.

If mutual trust hasn't yet been established, these contrasting moments can offer the opportunity to build trusting relationships. In the delicate personal conversation, authentic listening, sustained attention, understanding and willingness to help will signal to your colleague that you're available for them and that they can rely on you. In the analytical meeting, your clarity, focus and grip may well be the reason that your colleagues (or clients) decide they have faith in you because you're demonstrably capable and credible.

Without conscious thought and effort, however (and we have already established how neglected thinking time can be), it's difficult to make the flip from one state of mind to the other, with the potential hazard that we show up far more impactfully in one scenario and not the other. In the worst case, we could appear indifferent in both.

Tension 3: Conventional versus contemporary

Why should I swap the comfortable status quo for an uncertain new environment?

On hearing *Low* for the first time, executives at Bowie's record label, RCA, were confused at best, horrified at worst. So shocked and appalled was one executive (and so strong the inclination to keep Bowie in the location and style of his commercial triumph in America), he was reportedly heard to say: 'I'm gonna buy Bowie a house in Philadelphia and make him write *Young Americans II*.' As Tony Visconti later observed, though, 'He really didn't know David Bowie, did he?'[54]

With the benefit of hindsight, *Rolling Stone* magazine commented: '*Low* was underappreciated at the time, but now it's widely seen as a masterpiece.'[55]

The record company's indifferent reaction to *Low*'s groundbreaking sound and structure is illustrative of the third tension we face as we try to build trust: our attachment to the conventions that have previously made us successful, versus new ways of seeing. This tension is stretched further, given the perceived

---

54 'Album release: Low' (TheBowieBible, 29 November 2018), www.bowiebible.com/1977/01/14/album-release-low, accessed 31 October 2024

55 Rolling Stone, 'Readers' poll: The best David Bowie albums' (*Rolling Stone*, 16 January 2013), www.rollingstone.com/music/music-lists/readers-poll-the-best-david-bowie-albums-11994, accessed 1 November 2024

sensitivity of some of the topics involved when work-forces have increasingly diverse lives, experiences and attitudes.

Certain subject matters – including respecting pronouns, systemic racism, menopause and neurodiversity – may not have always been on a leader's traditional employee engagement radar. Subsequent and rapid changes in societal and cultural attitudes and access to far wider sources of information and perspective have brought them into focus. At times an event grabs multiple media headlines, without much advance warning or opportunity to consider the nuances and alternative views involved. The result can be leaders treading on eggshells because they lack the tools, knowledge or relatable experience to react constructively in the moment.

Instead, leaders opt to cling to the status quo rather than venturing into conversations for which there is no neat formula or assured outcome. Fear of being labelled, or handling sensitive issues clumsily, prevents them looking more closely at the system in which everyone exists but not everyone feels included. This might be accompanied by the hope that somebody else – perhaps a working group, a specialist or the board – will have the matter already on their agenda.

Unless this discomfort is faced, leaders are left feeling as isolated from those conversations as much as the very people they want to understand better, include and build trust with. Often leaders will choose inaction because they can't achieve perfection. We like the alternative: *imperfect action*. This at least creates the space where progress, deeper mutual understanding and empathy can emerge. We'll explore what this looks like in practice in our next chapter.

8
How To Stop The Neglect Of Building Trust

Like *Moon Safari*'s 'Sexy Boy', David Bowie's *Low* album had a big hit single. 'Sound and Vision' spent eleven weeks in the UK charts, peaking at number three.[56] The track's influence has continued to expand in the years since its release in 1977. Music producers throughout the 1980s tried to reproduce its distinctive drum sound. It has been streamed over 89,000,000 times on Spotify alone and has been covered by artists including Franz Ferdinand, Beck and Anna Calvi.

It's an impressive legacy for just over three minutes of music that discarded regular song structures

---

56 'David Bowie' (Official Charts), www.officialcharts.com/artist/19138/david-bowie, accessed 1 November 2024

and whose lyrics don't arrive until two-thirds of the way through.

Our observation, as we turn to what to do about the current neglect of building trust, is that this subject is currently dominated by one big idea, in the same way that a standout track can define our perception of an album.

The prevailing concept when we talk about the issues surrounding trust is *psychological safety*. The term is thought to have been coined originally in the 1950s by clinical psychologist Carl Rogers. He wrote about it in the context of creative work and described settings in which individuals could feel 'unconditional worth' rather than anxiety. The concept was incorporated into management theory by Edgar Schein and Warren Bennis, who defined it, among other things as, a climate 'which encourages provisional tries and which tolerates failure without retaliation, renunciation, or guilt.'[57]

In 1990 William Kahn cited psychological safety as a significant factor in engagement and disengagement at work.[58] Later, Amy Edmondson coined the

---

57 EH Schein and WG Bennis, *Personal and Organizational Change Through Group Methods: The laboratory approach* (John Wiley & Sons Ltd, 1965)

58 WA Kahn, 'Psychological conditions of personal engagement and disengagement at work', *The Academy of Management Journal*, 33/4 (1990), 692–724, https://doi.org/10.2307/256287

phrase *team psychological safety*, emphasising the idea that shared beliefs about it being OK to speak up with concerns, questions, ideas and alternative perspectives were an essential underpinning of a great team.[59]

Of course, in this atmosphere, trust has the ideal conditions to develop. As Edmondson puts it, a psychologically safe team climate is 'characterized by interpersonal trust and mutual respect in which people are comfortable being themselves'.

As well as trust and mutual respect, the benefits of psychological safety evidenced by Amy Edmondson and other academics and researchers are attractive:

- Greater motivation

- Wider inclusion

- Creativity

- Easier collaboration and learning

- Improved decision making

Perhaps the most eye-catching evidence is to be found in the previously mentioned Project Aristotle – Google's extensive 2012 study to discover what set

---

59 A Edmondson, 'Psychological safety and learning behavior in work teams', *Administrative Science Quarterly*, 44/2 (1999), 350–383, https://doi.org/10.2307/2666999

their top-performing teams apart. The initial analysis searched for patterns based on who was in teams – their levels of experience, preferences (eg for introversion and introversion), social connections outside work, diversity and team longevity – but found little that was conclusive.

The focus of the analysis switched to how the teams behaved and their group norms and habits. At this point, specific insights emerged. Psychological safety was identified as the common feature of the highest-performing teams in the organisation, with two dimensions particularly significant:

1. **Conversational turn taking:** each team member having a roughly equal share of voice (and using it)

2. **Social sensitivity:** individuals being tuned in to how others might be feeling and able to exercise emotional control over their own behaviour

The cumulative impact of this body of work means that creating psychologically safe spaces is a firm fixture in the leadership and cultural agendas of the organisations we spend time with. This makes sense, given the terrifying and complex scale of the challenges we need to face.

Why wouldn't we want thriving teams, collaborators and co-creators who feel comfortable and encouraged to bring their best contributions to work, without fear that they'll consequently be judged or held back? A space where there is unrestricted sharing of opinions and the ideas emerging just might contain the solution that nobody else has thought of yet.

However, in the day-to-day reality of leadership action, working on psychological safety is not straightforward. There is a danger that we're attracted to the buzzwords and clichés rather than to the in-depth work involved, just as we might prefer the melodies and choruses of a well-known song without staying curious and listening to the full album. As we expand our understanding of psychological safety, questions emerge:

- Why should I feel under pressure to *bring my whole self to work* if I'm a rather private person?

- Are we sure we want everyone to be free to make mistakes, when in some situations, carelessness might have serious consequences?

- What about the days when I desperately need time to myself to decompress or process rather than spending the day lavishing my emotional literacy on others?

- What is the difference between psychological safety and being in our comfort zone? Doesn't experience tell us that development, performance edge and innovation don't happen there?

Perhaps the challenge leaders face is that they are living in a moment where the positive impact of psychological safety is much spoken about as a concept, while the sleeves-rolled-back work of embedding it is harder to pin down. Our own recent research indicates that most organisations are on a journey to maturity in psychological safety and that progress tends to manifest in pockets of good practice, rather than in a linear way or through existing hierarchies.[60]

For us the first steps are based on a simple and fundamental act of building trust – the conversation.

Advocating for the power of conversations is not new to us. Published in October 2014, 5 *Conversations: How to transform trust, engagement and performance at work* by our colleagues at The Oxford Group, Nick Cowley and Nigel Purse, remains a flagship book and programme.[61]

We see positive and measurable results where clients focus their attention on conversations to build understanding, trust and connection.

---

60   The Oxford Group, 'Unlock innovation with psychological safety –
     Why it's time to face up to the challenges of a polarised world' (The
     Oxford Group, 13 May 2022), www.oxford-group.com/insights/
     unlock-innovation-with-psychological-safety-why-its-time-to-face-
     up-to-the-challenges-of-a-polarised-world, accessed 1 November
     2024
61   N Cowley and N Purse, 5 *Conversations: How to transform trust,
     engagement and performance at work* (Panoma Press, 2014)

CASE STUDY: Legal & General

The Insurance Customer Service division of Legal & General (a leading UK financial services provider) had focused for several years on creating a coaching culture. They wanted to build on this work and to develop a human-centred style of leadership to support wellbeing and employee engagement, while also delivering business outcomes.

The division set out with quantifiable aims to:

- Improve their survey scores relating to the coaching culture even further
- Improve their survey scores in the wider employee engagement survey
- Impact positively on more conventional contact-centre measures such as their customer satisfaction score (C-SAT)

The L&G Learning team incorporated the *5 Conversations* methodology as a key component of their Leading with Emotional Intelligence (LWEI) programme.

While all of the conversations are important, *establishing a trusting relationship* was viewed as foundational in creating the conditions for psychologically safe relationships and improved performance at work.

Gary Shewan, Learning & Development business partner at Legal & General, shared: 'I encourage all leaders to make the time to build real connections with their people; human-centred leadership isn't a skill – it's a mindset. Creating the right environment for your people to succeed is critical for any organisation, and this starts with the simple act of purposely creating time to connect and build trust.'

Peter Coats, Group Protection Academy manager, also added: 'Sometimes we are so busy with the day-to-day tasks that we forget the foundation of our role is to build trust with the colleagues that we lead. This needs to be a conscious and frequent activity. When you give something of yourself in a trust conversation, you will be amazed at the return you get on this investment.'

The outcome

From July 2020 to the end of 2023, the programme was delivered to 213 leaders at all levels of the organisations, from frontline supervisors through to C-suite executives. The LWEI programme had a considerable impact on how employees feel at work and, crucially, how they are performing.

In March 2021 L&G's Voice employee engagement survey demonstrated a marked improvement in confidence at work:

- Scores for 'I feel free to speak out without fear of negative consequences' rose from 64 to 74. In the control group of equivalent divisions not impacted by LWEI, the change was 57 to 68.
- Employee satisfaction increased from 74 to 78 in impacted teams.

The Coaching Survey conducted within Insurance Customer Service highlighted improvements year on year. Scores increased for:

- 'The level of trust you have in your line manager': 8.67/10 to 9.09/10.
- 'My line manager shows me genuine appreciation': from an already high score of 93.31 to 97.26.

In addition, there was a positive impact on employee retention, with staff turnover dropping from 9.1% in 2019 to 6.6% in 2020 (in contrast to 11.9% for L&G companywide in 2020).

A more positive employee experience is having a tangible impact on customer experience, with net promoter scores (NPS) rising across Insurance Customer Service, from 41 (October 2020) to 47 (August 2021).

One participant commented: 'I loved the interaction with other managers sharing best practices and challenges. Most importantly, the knowledge and tools I gained in building meaningful and trusting relationships with my colleagues has been invaluable.'

Programmes like L&G's LWEI pay back their investment with tangible, measurable effects on culture and performance. As we can hear from the participants' comments above, having formal time, space and support of colleagues, to pay attention to the action of building trust, is invigorating and positive.

We also know that, for all the reasons that we explored in our previous chapters, the moments when we make time for conversations aimed at building trust continue to be rare, can feel daunting, and may leave leaders feeling vulnerable or uncomfortable before the conversation starts, never mind during the interaction itself.

From our research into psychological safety, we realised that leaders lacked a practical framework that helps them prepare for, initiate and enjoy those open and open-minded conversations with their colleagues. As a result, we developed our HEAR model, based on four principles:

- Honesty

- Empathy

- Accuracy

- Respect

Each principle recognises the power of maintaining self-awareness *and* unbiased connection with the other person (as far as this is reasonably possible). This involves hearing yourself as well as hearing others, thereby creating the conditions for openness, curiosity and connection. As one of the respondents in our research said: 'Get to know the human, not the idea.'

There are two dimensions to the practice of HEAR: hearing yourself and hearing others. The successful application of HEAR as a framework for trust-building conversations demands that you work on both dimensions.

The HEAR model

Making a start

To start your HEAR practice, you HEAR yourself, paying attention to the following four steps.

1. Honesty

Be honest with how you are feeling and the role you want to play to guide your organisation.

In practice this means finding the appropriate language to describe how you feel about the conversation or the relationship. It may be enough to acknowledge this to yourself:

I'm feeling nervous about this conversation, and I know that I can draw on my experience and that it will have a positive impact on this relationship.

This will be a better melody to listen to than the jangling of your nerves. It could be that you want to articulate your feelings to the other person. You will always be more powerful if you can describe rather than demonstrate your emotions.

Look the other person in the eye and say clearly:

I haven't been looking forward to this conversation, but I'm glad we're here now.

This makes a far better impact than fidgeting and looking at your feet or fingernails, as the emotion makes itself felt anyway.

Being honest about the role you want to play in guiding your organisation is about the personal accountability you're taking for improving trust, contributing to a positive workplace, rather than waiting for some unspecified person to take action to stop neglect. If you feel committed and purposeful about this, acknowledge it to yourself. It's important.

2. Empathy

Show self-care with your experiences. You have value and others have value.

In Part Three we will look at the time leaders make for themselves. When you enact the empathy element of the HEAR model, you are acknowledging your own story, what it's taught you and the kind of leader it has enabled you to be. Empathy allows you to realise that you may not be scintillating and unforgettably witty in a specific conversation, but you can be present, thoughtful and non-judgemental, and you recognise that has strength and value.

Your experiences, relationships, trials, triumphs, indifferent moments, and good and bad days combine to make you unique in what you can offer. Treating yourself and the other person in the conversation as equally significant creates a climate for mutual understanding and authenticity.

3. Accuracy

Be accurate in understanding any biases that might be affecting your ability to invite and listen to others.

We understand that our bias towards *Low*, as one of the most important albums ever made, might lead us to tune out from someone who doesn't appreciate it or might make that claim for another album. That's a bias that is easy to recognise and can be acknowledged in a light-hearted way without too much concern for reputational damage.

Time spent on recognising, owning and understanding more subtle strata of bias that we have developed over time or through experience is less comfortable. Conscious reflection helps, with questions including:

- Why do I resist that idea or the person who represents that idea?
- What impact does it have on the prospect of us trusting each other?
- What restrictions does it place on me?
- What's a different way of looking at it?

A powerful step is turning up the background noise of bias so that we can listen to it, understand how it affects us, and then liberate ourselves from the distraction.

4. Respect

Respect your own views, which you have nurtured from years of experience. This is not about ignoring yourself.

Understanding and, where possible, stepping away from the containment that bias can bring doesn't mean undermining the value of our experience. To take a full and active part in a conversation, especially one aimed at building trust, we need to arrive with some confidence and belief in who we are and what we have to offer.

The second dimension of HEAR focuses on how you interact with the other person in the conversation.

1. Honesty

Be honest with your intention to listen and to share your own views.

There are two ways of being honest with your intention to listen:

- **Mindset:** Making a commitment to listening to and understanding the other person, not just waiting to speak. It helps to be actively curious, to suspend judgement and to make sure any immediate questions you ask are drawn from what the person said.

- **Behavioural:** Not talking over the other person, not finishing their sentences because you think you've spotted what they mean, not interrupting them and especially avoiding the interruption, *That reminds me of... me!* 'Oh I know what you mean because the same thing happened to me!' isn't empathy. It's interrupting.

A useful technique to use if you can hear the sound of your own voice and not the other person's is to think *WAIT?* WAIT is an acronym that stands for *Why am I talking?*

When you're sure the other person has finished what they want to say, meet their openness with similar generosity and share your perspective.

2. Empathy

Assume people are well intentioned, and opt to share their sincerity.

In an interview published by Al Jazeera's AJ+, Amarylis Fox – a former undercover CIA agent – summarised what she had learned from her extraordinary experience: 'Everyone believes they're the good guy.'

In conversation with another person, if you look for points of difference, political agendas and confirmation of your own bias, the chances are you'll find them. The fast-thinking parts of our brain are scanning for certainty, easy conclusions, reassurance that our assumptions are correct. We invite you to disrupt that pattern. Consciously use the starting point that the people you are in conversation with have the best of intentions and are operating from a place that makes sense to them, just as you are. First and foremost, a successful conversation allows you to understand, more than you did before, about what that place is like and why it matters to that person.

3. Accuracy

Be accurate in hearing the facts – what they are saying rather than what you feel about what they are saying.

After a recent meeting with a client's leadership team, we were surprised to hear one of the participants say, 'It will be much easier to plan and make decisions when the MD has set out this year's strategic priorities.' We were confused. We had heard the MD talk about four areas of focus for the twelve months ahead, and we felt clear about overall direction and what was most important.

How do two or more people have a different experience of what is said in a meeting? The reason could be as simple as language and structure. If you're waiting to hear the managing director say explicitly, 'Here are the four priorities for the year', and you don't hear that precise language, perhaps clarity is lost for you. It may be that you generally prefer specific information, and the other person is sketching out the big picture.

It's also possible that other factors are at play. If you don't support the direction set out, or if you can't see where your role and added value lie, or there are uncomfortable implications for you, or you don't believe the managing director is skilful in setting priorities, then you will interpret what is said through the frame of your feelings rather than taking time to understand what is being said and what the individual means.

Given our oversaturated working lives, hearing with accuracy takes conscious effort. We need to be fully present and endeavouring to listen without prejudice. Faced with this challenge, we recommend *actively wondering* – in other words, setting out to understand what the individual you are hearing means to say. Questions that are helpful here could be:

- What does this individual mean when they say that?
- Why is this important to them?
- What interference might be getting in my way?

4. Respect

Respect others' views. Where is the common ground, and where are the different perspectives? Respecting is not the same as agreeing.

Once you are genuinely hearing what your conversational partner says, there's an important distinction to be made as you respond. You may not like what you hear, but revealing that won't result in lasting trust.

Trust will flourish if you acknowledge what the other person has said, give it as much weight as your own point of view and open yourself up to the possibilities their opinion brings. Trust grows when you ask questions rather than jumping directly into criticism or defence. Trust is encouraged when you reflect back what the person has said, check your understanding and ask them to tell you more. It doesn't falter then when you say *I see things differently* in a spirit of mutual respect.

Using HEAR is active. It's a practice that might seem effortful and self-conscious at first, and it becomes easy and rewarding as you make it habitual. It is useful for moments of introspection before you start a conversation. It helps you to ground yourself and to be comfortable with yourself and your leadership role.

Reflecting ahead of time on someone's positive qualities means you can approach the conversation with a certain level of confidence and equanimity. HEAR is also a useful guide to maintaining a positive presence throughout the conversation and for reviewing it afterwards.

As with all our neglected acts, the key is to pause and then prioritise these moments of human connection. There will always be a reason not to do this – genuinely hearing others won't often feel urgent or demand your attention. That is, until something goes wrong and you're left cursing the fact that you didn't develop trust as an asset in your team. Trust-enhancing conversations are like the gorgeous, underrated album track you discover when you sit and listen to the whole record and realise what you've been missing.

Today's hectic, lean-team environments can – and do – lead to tension and pressure to get tasks done as quickly and efficiently as possible. It's easy in those circumstances to forget that teams are made up of individuals that may have widely differing needs, opinions or concerns.

Knowing what those differences are lays the groundwork for you to offer the support and the challenge that people need. You can reduce the risk of a team member feeling unhappy, unwilling or unmotivated to carry out the task, while increasing the likelihood that they stretch themselves or take on a new opportunity because they trust your intention and judgement and feel secure.

The power of paying attention to trust extends beyond immediate teams and collaborators to your boss, interconnected colleagues, stakeholders, customers, suppliers and wider networks.

Alongside integrating our HEAR model into your practice as a leader, we have also created a selection of questions that we know are useful in establishing a relationship of trust. You'll find those questions outlined in the table below.

Questions to establish a trusting relationship

Question type	Question examples
Opening questions	• What would you most like to ask me that will help you to understand me better?
Questions that reveal what they value	• What's really important to you at work? • What do you feel most strongly about? • What are you most passionate about?
Questions that indicate how they view themselves	• What do you consider your greatest strength? What are you most proud of? • What do you think is your greatest limitation? What do you want to be known for? • What is it that you really stand for?
Questions that show what's important to them in their relationships with others	• What's important to you in building a relationship with someone? What matters most to you when trusting others? • When do you tend to feel most badly let down by a colleague? What sorts of things damage a relationship for you? • To what extent do you tend to open up to others at work? How easily do you trust others? • What one thing could I tell you that would help you to trust me?

Question type	Question examples
Questions that highlight what they need from work	• Tell me about a good day at work. What gives you most satisfaction at work? What energises you?
	• Tell me what a bad day at work looks like. What causes you most anxiety at work?
	• What causes you to lose sleep at night?
	• Which emotions do you experience most often at work?
Open questions for when you've both revealed more in response to specific questions	• What one question could I ask you that would enable me to really understand you?
Questions for when you know the other person well	• What one thing about you can you tell me that might be helpful for me to know that I don't already know?
	• Do you have any unrealised ambitions?
	• What do you most value about working here?
	• What one thing would you change about working here and why? What would you like to be most remembered for?

As we close this chapter, we would encourage you to stop neglecting trust for another, more personal reason. However conscientious, dedicated and energetic a leader you are, you need to pay attention to yourself. If you continue to attack tasks at an accelerated and unsustainable rate, your relationships with others won't keep pace, and you will find yourself over-worked, isolated and trapped in a limit cycle.

Unless we consciously create an atmosphere of trust, we neglect our own basic needs and, as a result, our leadership potential.

Our third neglected act of leadership, the neglect of self, follows. Let's take some time for ourselves in the final part of this book.

PART THREE
THE NEGLECT OF SELF

9

The Story Of *My 21st Century Blues* By Raye

I n June 2021, Raye tweeted, 'I'm done with being a polite pop star.'

In the same year, she parted ways with her record company Polydor and began working independently, releasing her debut album *My 21st Century Blues* in February 2023.

In 2024, she broke records at the BRIT Awards, winning six awards, the highest number by any artist in a single night and became the first woman to win the Songwriter of the Year award. She won a MOBO award for best female artist and an Ivor Novello award for Songwriter of the Year.[62] In 2025, she has been nominated for two Grammys for Best New Artist and Songwriter of the Year.[63] Tracks from her debut album *My 21st Century Blues* have been streamed over 1.3 billon times.[64] This dizzying personal success and recognition seemed very far away during the 'polite popstar' years.

Growing up, Raye had been single-minded about what she wanted to be. She wrote her first song at age seven, and at fourteen, fulfilled her ambition to attend the BRIT School, a performing arts institution with alumni including Adele and Amy Winehouse. While she was there, she was devoted to her song writing, giving up evenings and weekends to take every opportunity to develop her work.

She signed a four-album deal with Polydor at age seventeen in 2014. 'When you think, "I want to be an artist," there are a few things you think of, the first thing being: album," she told *The New York Times* in

---

62 T Garcia, 'Ivor Novello Awards 2024 winners list: Raye wins Songwriter of the Year, Paul McCartney Presents Fellowship to Bruce Springsteen', *Variety* (24 May 2024), https://variety.com/2024/music/news/ivor-novello-awards-winners-list-raye-1236015145/, accessed 16 January 2025

63 B Gracie, '2025 GRAMMYs nominations: record of the year nominees', *GRAMMYs* (8 November 2024), www.grammy.com/news/2025-grammys-nominations-record-of-the-year, accessed 16 January 2025

64 Raye (@rayeupdates) 'My 21st Century Blues received 476 MILLION streams in 2024' (January 2025), www.instagram.com/rayeupdates/p/DEUe1AWRNdC/, accessed 16 January 2025

2023.[65] However, this defining artistic moment was not forthcoming.

Instead, her talent and skills were directed toward writing songs for other artists including Beyoncé, John Legend, Little Mix and Charlie XCX, and collaborations on commercially orientated dance tracks. 'From a business perspective, they decided for me that I was this, and this was all I would ever be,' she told *The New York Times*.[66]

Her work ethic continued, but her frustration at having no control, no space and limited opportunity was growing. It was the news that the label would not be releasing an album with her that catalysed her game-changing tweets in February of 2023.

'I've done everything they asked – I switched genres, I worked seven days a week… I want to make my album now.'

Having ended her relationship with her record company and chosen to work with an independent distributor, Raye finally had time for herself.

The making of *My 21st Century Blues* was not straightforward despite her creative freedom. She needed to

---

65 S Hans, 'Raye, tired of music's waiting game, releases an album at last', *The New York Times* (2 March 2023), www.nytimes.com/2023/02/03/arts/music/raye-my-21st-century-blues.html, accessed 16 January 2025

66 Ibid.

take material she had been accumulating for seven years and shape it into the music she wanted to make, breaking out of the constraints that other people had fashioned for her.

The songs on the album draw from raw personal experience including disordered eating, substance abuse and sexual assault. Her stories are told with honesty and authenticity. 'There's things on there that some of my closest friends don't even know about me,' she explained to *Rolling Stone* magazine. 'Even though it's difficult and tricky at times, I do believe art is about being ruthlessly honest.'[67]

Raye was motivated by her growing personal conviction about who she was: 'Artistry really stems from your identity. An artist is conviction and having a perspective that you identify with and you back and you love 100%,' she told *Paper* magazine in February 2023.[68] Having navigated emotional intensity, musical innovation, decision making and commercial risks, Raye has described reaching a powerful place. 'All of this music has been some form of medicine to me.

---

67 L O'Neill, 'Raye: in full control', *Rolling Stone* (January 2025), www.rollingstone.co.uk/music/features/raye-in-full-control-escapism-25706/, accessed 16 January 2025

68 C Bell, 'Raye's perfect blues', *Paper* (9 February 2023), www.papermag.com/raye-my-21st-century-blues#rebelltitem27, accessed 16 January 2025

I feel liberated now,' she revealed in an interview with *Nylon* in February 2024.[69]

The experience of making *My 21st Century Blues* also seems to have defined what Raye needed to sustain her as an artist. This includes her family – her parents gave up their jobs to manage her full time. 'Before I involved my parents in my career, I was so lost and I was really not doing well. I need people around me who really care about me, who have my best interests at heart and know my boundaries,' she explained to *Elle* magazine.[70]

A close circle of collaborators and partners has also been vital. Ian Dutt the UK MD of The Orchard, her distribution partner, said, 'The most important thing was to build an environment around Raye that was empathetic, inclusive and creative. It gave her the freedom and confidence to make the decisions she wanted to make.'[71]

She has also spoken about her faith as an important source of strength. *My 21st Century Blues* ends with

---

69 M Peay, 'Raye explicity speaks her mind on debut album, "My 21st Century Blues"', *Nylon* (20 February 2024), www.nylon.com/entertainment/raye-my-21st-century-blues-album-independent, accessed 16 January 2025

70 S Mahanty, 'Raye of light', *Elle* (3 April 2024), www.elle.com/uk/life-and-culture/culture/a60303935/raye-interview/, accessed 16 January 2025

71 A Paine, 'Escape plan: Raye's artist services team on the ascent of a "global superstar"', *MusicWeek* (22 February 2023), www.musicweek.com/interviews/read/escape-plan-raye-s-artist-services-team-on-the-ascent-of-a-global-superstar/087384, accessed 16 January 2025

a lush and hopeful final track 'Buss it Down', which looks to the future with confidence and certainty. This celebratory sign off marks the end of a profound adventure which began when Raye stopped compromising her work and herself by trying to please everyone else. By refusing to tolerate the limitations that others placed on her and taking time for herself, she began to fulfil her incredible potential.

What we can learn from Raye about taking time for ourselves

For us this comes down to three factors:

1. **Making time for ourselves is not self-indulgence – it is essential so that we can be purposeful and understand the contribution that we are capable of.** Whether that means time to recognise who we want to be and what drives us, to learn from experience, to breathe out and start thinking straight or to decompress and process the fallout of a difficult situation, the ensuing benefits ripple out far beyond us. When we step back into the leadership space, clear-headed, renewed and ready to move forward, our impact will be powerful.

2. **Genuine self-awareness, self-development and self-care may well involve some discomfort as well as respite.** Examining our experience and being honest, especially in the face of adversity

is an act of courage. When we look inside rather than outside and take responsibility for ourselves, we might discover what we really need. Even more radically, we might allow ourselves to have it.

3. **It starts with us.** From an intolerable situation, an incredible piece of art emerged, and global success followed. This was only possible because Raye was willing to recognise and confront the cycle she was trapped in, and she strove for something far better for herself, and, as she progressed, to define what she needed to do her best work. If we choose to, it's possible for each of us to take a deliberate step to make time for ourselves.

Received wisdom tells us that the basics of taking time for ourselves involves walks in nature, pleasant social contact or a sense of purpose beyond ourselves. It's about finding the prescription that works for you.

One simple exercise we use in our work with leaders is inviting them to take a sheet of paper, divide it into two columns, take some time to think and then write down the things that nourish them on one side and the things that detract from their wellbeing on the other. What is surprising isn't so much what people write down in their lists, but the fact that so many tell us they've *never* taken the time to think about this before.

My 21st Century Blues was born from a moment of personal crisis, and it became epic in its ambition. We advocate that acting to stop the neglect of self should happen *long before* things fall apart, or you get to the cusp of burn-out. Addressing this neglect should also be a positive, purposeful choice for leaders, whatever it is in your world you want to change.

Is it selfish to understand what you need and want?

No. Will taking those moments for yourself prove productive?

Yes. Why?

This is how and when you can become clear about yourself and your aims, and allow yourself to think about your vision for the future. It's about having more energy, creativity and resilience to work alongside your collaborators to deliver the extraordinary. In the forthcoming chapters, we will discover why we neglect ourselves and how we can take simple practical steps to embed the habits that lead to remarkable results.

10
Why We Neglect Ourselves

Before we go any further, we want to be perfectly clear as to our meaning when we refer to *self*. We're not talking about your ego, your brand, your next career move or your social media status.

We are talking about *you*.

We've already discussed the intensity of working life – the fierce demands, the irreconcilable priorities, the trade-offs, the impairment of our thinking time and the challenges of building trust with others. Perhaps we shouldn't be surprised, therefore, that leaders so often put themselves, their wellbeing and their needs low on their ever expanding to-do list. Otherwise, they'd look selfish, wouldn't they? Surely the way to add value is to address the demands of the day, to motivate your team, to understand what your stakeholders want and to deliver results? Writer and consultant Victor Lipman endorsed this: 'I'd argue that as a leader you're setting the best example when you focus most on others and only minimally on yourself.'[72]

Naturally, when your team members feel that you go the extra mile to empower and enrich them, this signals excellent leadership skills that encourage people to follow you. We wouldn't argue with this in principle, and we also acknowledge that to sustain this style of leadership you need self-belief, self-reliance and self-awareness. However, none of this is a given, and even our most balanced and most generous selves need space, thought and care.

It has never been easier to find out more about yourself. For example:

- Psychometric evaluations, tested for reliability and validity, will offer you insight into your preferences, your levels of emotional intelligence, how you react under stress.

- Your colleagues can offer you 360-degree feedback online.

---

72 V Lipman, 'It's not about you. (The best leaders focus on others.)' (*Forbes*, 17 September 2012), www.forbes.com/sites/ victorlipman/2012/09/17/its-not-about-you-the-best-leaders-focus-on-others, accessed 1 November 2024

- Leadership programmes will invite you to think about your values, your personal manifesto, your leadership shadow.

- Personalised devices can update you on your sleep, your daily steps, your heart rate.

The availability of data, tools and materials that help us know more about ourselves has never been greater, yet many leaders perceive spending time on themselves as unnecessary or even indulgent. As a result, it's often neither a priority nor a practice.

Once again, understanding some of the influences that contribute to the neglect of self at global, organisational and individual levels can offer insight into how we might halt the neglect, as we'll address in this chapter.

Global perspective

In April 2021 *The New York Times* published an article that piqued our curiosity and prompted us to think more deeply about the impact that a worldwide pandemic had on people's sense of self. The headline was: 'There's a Name for the Blah You're Feeling: It's Called Languishing'.[73]

---

73 A Grant, 'There's a name for the blah you're feeling: It's called languishing' (*The New York Times*, 19 April 2021), www.nytimes. com/2021/04/19/well/mind/covid-mental-health-languishing. html, accessed 1 November 2024

Languishing

During (and since) the Covid pandemic, a head-spinning combination of uncertainty, economic instability, shifting regulations, remote work challenges, health and safety concerns, tough trading conditions and financial pressures left many business leaders feeling overwhelmed and unsure both about the future and about themselves. When the author raised the concept of languishing, it struck a chord.

The article defined languishing as 'stagnation and emptiness, muddling through, looking at life through a foggy windshield'.[74] The author presented languishing as the middle child of mental health, describing it as 'the void between depression and flourishing – the absence of wellbeing'.[75]

It was the original research paper by Corey Keyes that first set out the concept.[76] Keyes posited that there's a spectrum, at the far end of which reside pathological mental health conditions (eg depression). At the opposite end we find *flourishing*. Here we live fulfilled lives, feeling safe and happy, surrounded by similarly purpose-driven people in the pursuit of

---

74 Ibid.
75 Ibid.
76 CLM Keyes et al., 'Change in level of positive mental health as a predictor of future risk of mental illness', *American Journal of Public Health*, 100/12 (2010), 2366–71, https://doi.org/10.2105/AJPH.2010.192245

what we love doing best. This is the space where we play to our strengths and use all our gifts to create a positive impact.

In the middle of this spectrum sits languishing. It's not a pathological condition. It's just 'meh'. That feeling of trying to get through the day without any sense of joy or achievement.

It seems that in our post-pandemic hangover, feelings of languishing have become increasingly prevalent as people grapple with the long-lasting challenges of isolation, uncertainty and stress.

Keyes' findings underscore the importance of recognising and addressing feelings of languishing, as they can serve as early warning signs of declining mental health and wellbeing.

The *New York Times* article was published as we emerged into an unclear post-pandemic future, and many people recognised the symptoms in themselves. Interestingly, at this time many organisations had begun to focus on developing a greater sensitivity in understanding the complexities of mental health. Facing a global health crisis brought about a myriad of stressors and challenges for many individuals, no doubt intensifying the recognition that greater awareness, fewer taboos and better dialogue around mental health formed positive progress.

As a leadership consultancy, we've pondered this sense of languishing and seen it among clients we work with. It's plausible that the incessant need to compare ourselves to the curated images portrayed on social media diminishes our sense of inspiration and stifles our capacity for joy. Perhaps leaders spend too much time measuring themselves against others and feel inadequate as a result? In so doing, they avoid the chance for self-reflection, along with the more balanced and insightful view self-reflection can bring.

Perhaps the sense that our global challenges are existential and insurmountable makes us feel small and ineffective? This leads to the question, *Why spend time on ourselves when there's nothing we can do that makes a difference anyway?*

The rise of wellness

According to McKinsey, the global wellness industry – encompassing better health, fitness, nutrition, appearance and mindfulness – is valued at $1.5 trillion, with an expected annual growth rate of 5–10%.[77] All this is cleverly marketed to make us feel we're not doing enough or could be achieving even more.

---

77 S Callaghan et al., 'Feeling good: The future of the $1.5 trillion wellness market' (McKinsey & Company, 8 April 2021), www.mckinsey.com/industries/consumer-packaged-goods/our-insights/feeling-good-the-future-of-the-1-5-trillion-wellness-market, accessed 1 November 2024

According to the same research by McKinsey, 79% of respondents consider wellness important, with 42% ranking it as a top priority. It seems that the data contradicts the contention that we do in fact neglect ourselves, suggesting that we have a strong interest in self-improvement.

However, the same research reveals that consumers worldwide don't experience the expected improvements in wellness. In fact, most (except consumers in China and Brazil) report stagnation or decline.

In 2019 the World Health Organization officially classified *burnout* as an occupational phenomenon in the International Classification of Diseases.[78] While studies differ on the extent of burnout's increase since then, there is consensus that we're at a higher risk of it in the workplace. In light of this, there's persuasive evidence to suggest that we're not dedicating enough positive time to ourselves.

It's a paradox that hasn't yet been resolved: people haven't become the 'self' they aspire to be, despite the booming wellness industry. There are countless apps and online videos for every aspect of wellness. Despite hyper-awareness that we should be healthier and take care of ourselves, there's a pervasive sense of

---

78 WHO, 'Burn-out an "occupational phenomenon": International Classification of Diseases' (World Health Organization, 28 May 2019), www.who.int/news/item/28-05-2019-burn-out-an-occupational-phenomenon-international-classification-of-diseases, accessed 1 November 2024

dissatisfaction because we're not making it a successful part of our daily lives.

Surprisingly – or perhaps not – according to WHO's findings, some organisations view exhaustion as a mark of success, which is an outdated and counterproductive perspective. This mindset isn't uncommon, however, among leaders who believe that busyness equates to status.

Does the rise of wellness, with its constant innovation, new trends, rising stars and digital dominance, represent progress in how we pay the right amount of attention to ourselves? Or, with the abundance of wellbeing options and information available, is it all too easy to become dissatisfied when we feel we're not doing the right thing or when the latest trend doesn't deliver immediate results?

In the past – before internet access – we once relied on health professionals for guidance. Today people often self-diagnose due to the wealth of information online. However, while this can lead to making informed decisions, it's equally likely we are influenced by misinformation. The rise of the 'worried well' – people constantly in search of answers to perceived problems or possibilities without satisfactory solutions – is a twenty-first-century phenomenon. While self-absorption might be on the rise, we're more likely to have a strong sense that it doesn't lead to positive outcomes. We therefore either neglect what we genuinely need to be at our best, or we give up before we've seen a difference. This makes it far more challenging to overcome our disappointment before we refocus and try again.

Organisational perspective

The global perspective suggests a confused picture in the way we think about ourselves. In organisational life, the ambiguity continues.

Blurred lines

It's worth considering where and when we might begin to pay attention to ourselves. How much does this action belong in a work setting rather than being purely personal? To make this question trickier: it can often be difficult for leaders to discern when work ends and personal time begins.

Research by Microsoft conducted in 2022 found that the average number of global meetings per week for Microsoft Teams users had increased by 153%. Moreover, as we mentioned earlier, overlapping (double-booked) meetings rose by 46% per person in 2023.[79]

---

79 Microsoft, 'Great Expectations: Making hybrid work *work*' (Work Trend Index Annual Report, 16 March 2022), www.microsoft.com/en-us/worklab/work-trend-index/great-expectations-making-hybrid-work-work, accessed 1 November 2024

With this high level of demand on leaders' time and their tendency to remain busy, it's worth asking yourself: where does the creeping expansion of *my* working day end?

One of our most popular workshops is 'How to lead hybrid teams'. When we run it, leaders want to talk and talk and talk and talk about the hybrid model they work with – the opportunities, the flexibility, the difficulties, the frustrations, the impossibility of keeping everyone happy and, not least of which, where the boundaries should be drawn between work and home.

Remote working isn't a new development. Pre-pandemic, many organisations worldwide had already explored flexible working and successfully managed teams spread across different continents and time zones, enabled by rapidly improving technology. It's just that the numbers of office-based employees splitting their time between HQ and home has multiplied. The truth is that figuring out the best conventions, habits and behaviours remains an ongoing process.

For many people this situation creates welcome flexibility, since it offers the opportunity to work at times that suit their circumstances and their energy. The downside for some is the blurred line. How do you know when you're at home or at work if the location is the same and the technology means you can log on, be contacted and produce output at any time of day?

With the traditional commute on the decline, so is the natural buffer between work and home life, along with useful travel time to unwind and reflect. The onset of hybrid working leaves people telling us that they now struggle to fully disconnect from work, leading to a constant temptation to stay connected via their devices. At one time, consultants and HR departments would talk a lot about work–life balance. That's become work–life blending. If leaders are unable to make the distinction, the immediate risk is two-fold:

1. How can they ever be certain about when their work actually stops?

2. What do they do about their compelling obligation to be constantly available?

One of the leaders we work with typically sent her team a host of emails on a Sunday night. For her it was a quiet time, when she could gather her thoughts and prepare and plan for the week ahead. 'I certainly don't expect my team to respond,' she said. 'I'd prefer that they didn't, although sometimes they do.'

What was missing was the conversation that clarified this expectation. Without it, the signal she sent her team was that the boss is working on Sundays, and so perhaps the team should be too. While this behaviour is often unintentional, a leader's desire to appear available and significant at all times can create pressure for those looking up to them.

Another of our clients was a high-performing team leader. She was a dedicated and hardworking individual who held herself to high standards and was leading a relatively new team. As part of a development programme, her team were invited to contribute to a 360-degree feedback process for her. One of her team members bravely pointed out that she was always the first one in and the last one out of the office. They commented that each morning she headed straight to her desk without saying hello and rarely took breaks or lunch, working beyond her prescribed hours.

This behaviour made everyone else feel as though they were expected to work in the same way, even though not everyone felt inclined to follow her example. They no longer felt they had permission to have a breather or engage in casual chats with each other, which limited the quality of team relationships and the levels of comfort and enjoyment they experienced at work. Our client was shocked by this feedback. She hadn't realised the impact that her behaviour created, imagining it was simply a personal choice. The next day she went into the office, greeted each of her team and made them all a cup of tea.

The power of the leader to bring clarity and reason to this situation brings us to another organisational dimension in the neglect of self: the ideal of the authentic leader.

Authentic leadership

Like Raye we spend time collaborating with talented people. We have many conversations about leadership, what it entails, what's effective and what isn't. We notice shifts in the language we use. *Charismatic leadership*, for example, seems to have fallen out of favour, especially given the negative behaviour exhibited by some leaders who might have been considered to fall into that category. As we've already discussed, there's also been a decline in deference towards authority figures, with leaders challenged to earn respect rather than assume it comes automatically with a certain position or title.

In today's complex world, leaders are expected to resolve paradoxes, devise strategies for seemingly unsolvable problems, make decisions when there's no compelling right answer, create psychologically safe environments, and above all, perform at an unattainable pace. Moreover, amid these expectations, there's a call for leaders to be authentic in all that they do.

We often hear that leaders should show vulnerability but what does that mean? Raye's raw and emotional performance as she explores moments of profound personal challenge is extraordinary, but our leaders aren't working in her artistic context. Being vulnerable is still an unclear and potentially uncomfortable space.

At the core of this call for authenticity lies a recognition of the importance of human connection, especially at a time where work is increasingly decentralised. People appreciate leaders who are genuine, honest and willing to admit when they don't have all the answers. This shift – away from the notion that leaders must have all the authority, expertise and insight – is significant.

What are we really asking of leaders when we talk about authenticity?

It's a difficult question, particularly when individuals may prefer to keep aspects of themselves private. The demand for full disclosure can feel blunt and unreasonable.

While the call for authenticity in leadership is well intentioned, it also demands nuance, particularly in a society where judgement can be swift and pervasive, and when offence might be quickly taken.

In attempting to be authentic, people walk a fine line, wary of what is acceptable in the eyes of others. In an increasingly polarised world, our own research suggests that topics perceived as edgier are often avoided because of the possible discomfort involved. It's hardly surprising, therefore, that leaders tell us that they're tentative about expressing their authentic selves because they can never really be sure what is helpful, appropriate and safe.

Consequently, when the corporate zeitgeist urges leaders to be vulnerable and authentic, the intricacies are often oversimplified, making it preferable to switch attention well away from the self wherever possible.

In the programmes and coaching sessions we run with executives and leaders, we often create a space for individuals to reflect on their values, goals and desired leadership style. We usually find that people appreciate this opportunity and enjoy delving into it. They also tell us that they rarely take the time to engage in such introspection. While the demand for authenticity exists, many individuals struggle to find – or make – the time to work out what this really means for them, unless they're in a dedicated development setting.

Personal perspective

Perhaps you've been nodding along as you've reached this point because you recognise some aspects of yourself? We hope this prompts you to ask yourself:

- Why is there often a sense of guilt associated with spending time on myself?

- Why does the time I spend on self-improvement or self-care still leave me languishing?

- Why is it perceived as less legitimate to prioritise personal growth over attending routine meetings that could easily be delegated?

It's not unheard of for our programme participants to express hesitation about taking action or sharing new ideas with their teams because, as one put it, 'I don't want everyone to say, *Oh, who's been on a course?*' In our opinion (and naturally we'd prefer everyone to advocate for their experience!), this self-consciousness is rooted in a fear of being perceived as selfish, ambitious or egotistical rather than recognising that the attention paid to the self brings potential benefits for both the individual and the organisation.

Despite the evident importance of leadership development, a recurring trend is to attempt to streamline or accelerate the process, often due to the perceived time constraints of busy individuals. *Can we do it in a shorter amount of time?* is an often repeated request, because leaders are seen as *very busy people,* and *their diaries are challenging.* Within that context, individuals naturally struggle to carve out time for self-development, despite acknowledging its importance.

This limit cycle, wherein individuals recognise the value of investing in themselves yet struggle to prioritise it amid competing demands, begs the question:

Do you allow other tasks to take precedence over your own growth and development, and if so, why?

Revenge procrastination bedtime

This phenomenon originated in China in response to the common nine/six pattern (where a person works nine hours a day for six days a week). Operating like this within major corporations is often seen as prestigious, conferring professional success and societal status. However, this reward often comes at a significant personal cost.

The resulting *revenge procrastination bedtime* phenomenon means in essence that, after a long and stressful workday, individuals forego much-needed sleep to carve out time for personal activities. Whether that's reading, watching a TV series or exercising, they will sacrifice sleep to reclaim a sense of autonomy over their time.

This behaviour has gained attention on platforms such as TikTok, where individuals share their experiences of stealing moments for themselves during late hours. However, the consequences can be severe. Sleep deprivation is considered one of the most detrimental factors to overall wellbeing, outweighing even poor diet and lack of exercise. Over time, the cumulative effects of sleep deprivation can lead to impaired cognitive function, physical debilitation and overall health decline.[80] None of these are considered good leadership traits.

We know that the consensus around wellbeing is that we need:

- Meaningful relationships and connections
- Time to think and recharge
- A rekindled sense of playfulness
- Uninterrupted absorption in activities that we enjoy

As with each of our neglected acts, if only it were that simple.

Our challenge to you is to give yourself permission to focus on:

- Who you are
- Where you want to go
- What you need to get there in a way that creates results for you

We chose to highlight the story behind *My 21st Century Blues* with its journey of personal exploration

---

80 E Suni and A Dimitriu, 'What is "revenge bedtime procrastination"?' (Sleep Foundation, 8 December 2023), www.sleepfoundation. org/sleep-hygiene/revenge-bedtime-procrastination, accessed 1 November 2024

and ultimately redemption and optimism for a reason. The album that Raye made allowed her to place her story and her perspective at the centre once she stopped tolerating a situation that was limiting her talent and her career.

In the following chapter we explore the tensions that lead to our procrastination in paying attention to ourselves. Following that, we offer some practical suggestions on how to stop perpetuating habits that don't help, as well as identify and embed habits that do.

11
Time For Self:
Three Tensions

J ust as we considered the reasons we are prone to neglect thinking time and building trust, this chapter will examine the tensions that prevent us from focusing on ourselves.

One of our clients – let's call them Jo – was a busy leader, who was constantly on the go and struggled to prioritise time for self. Exercise felt like a luxury, and healthy meals were sacrificed for convenience, working through lunch and at times into the evening. Despite recognising the value of practices such as meditation, integrating them into the daily or weekly routine felt impossible. The constant busyness took a toll, leaving Jo drained and unfocused. Jo knew a change was needed, but the drastic measures required seemed overwhelming and so the status quo was maintained.

Jo's example is not untypical of many of the leaders we work with, where time for self isn't a priority but a neglected act (more on Jo's story later).

Our other neglected acts – taking time to think and building trust – are not neglected because leaders believe they're a bad or questionable thing to do. The benefits for action on both are clear and backed by thorough research.

Our firm belief is that tackling our third identified neglected act – the neglect of self – is *equally essential*. As we explored in our previous chapter, though, the climate around paying attention to oneself is filled with confusion and contradiction.

We're becoming more aware of reasons why people struggle to thrive, and we have a growing vocabulary to articulate these challenges. While organisations increasingly address mental health and wellbeing and, in response, offer a plethora of options to enhance personal growth, burnout rates remain on the rise. Languishing is widespread, and many of our clients admit that they rarely prioritise time for self or reflection.

There are also fundamental questions about how to incorporate time for yourself into a busy week, not only due to time constraints but also because of a lack of clarity:

- Is this a legitimate work-related task or strictly personal?

- Who am I doing this for?

- What exactly should I or could I be doing?

- Isn't it all terribly self-indulgent anyway?

What prevents us taking time for ourselves

This leads to our first tension that prevents individuals from prioritising themselves: the uncomfortable emotions that mean it just doesn't feel quite right.

Tension 1: The guilt factor

If I take time for me, does that mean I think I'm more important than everyone else, and what will other people think?

Mixed emotions about the idea of paying attention to ourselves prevent us recognising the compelling reasons why it should be a clear leadership responsibility, whether that is for business, team or personal reasons. As a result, a major dilemma leaders face is the sense of guilt. How can they justify putting themselves at the centre when there are so many other demands for their attention, when others need them?

Surely, they're supposed to be capable, strong and adaptable? What are they doing wrong if they're not? Add to this the concern about how others might perceive them. The last thing any leader wants is for their team to think they don't care, wondering why their boss is out taking a leisurely stroll while they're working frantically in the office.

Let's examine the arguments for taking time to prioritise yourself, or what we might call *proper selfishness*:

- Giving constantly without refuelling your own energy depletes you both physically and emotionally. When you reach a point of exhaustion, or even burnout, your ability to positively contribute to your role or support your team diminishes significantly.

- Pressing on when you're tired and uninspired makes it harder to focus, make decisions or get tasks done efficiently. This impacts not only your productivity but also that of your colleagues and collaborators.

- When workplace relationships are strained due to depleted empathy, you become less open to new ideas in daily interactions. This limits your ability to connect with team members and colleagues across the organisation and beyond.

- Putting others consistently ahead of yourself can lead to lower self-esteem, making you feel less valued and less deserving of attention. As we explored in the HEAR model, you can't hear others effectively unless you can hear yourself.

- In the melee of life, work and uncertain futures, there's danger that you can lose yourself, leaving you disconnected from your purpose and your interests, causing you to gradually lose sight of who you are.

In the face of those considerations, time for yourself sounds less indulgent. Compelling research published in 2022 explores the question *Does self-care make you a better leader?*[81] It concludes that self-caring leaders were found to report more staff care than those low on self-care. Their employees perceive higher staff care and report lower strain and better health. This evidence gives us cause to seriously challenge the guilt factor that so many of us may have experienced.

However, even if you absolve yourself of the negative connotations and resolve to be more proactive about paying attention to yourself, you still face the question of what time for yourself actually involves.

---

81 K Klug et al., 'Does self-care make you a better leader? A Multisource study linking leader self-care to health-oriented leadership, employee self-care, and health', *International Journal of Environmental Research and Public Health*, 19/11 (2022), https://doi.org/10.3390/ijerph19116733

Tension 2: The self-what factor

What and who am I spending time on, exactly?

We attach many words to the prefix 'self', usually loaded in their meaning:

- Self-orientation, self-interest, self-centredness, self-indulgence – not so good
- Self-awareness, self-starting, self-confidence – perhaps more positive
- Self-care. Notice your reaction. What does it mean for you?

When we advocate paying more attention to yourself and avoiding the risks that can crystallise out of neglect, which 'self' do we mean exactly? Before pinpointing that, it feels important to dispense with the pejoratives that surround self-care, because the consequences of ignoring or belittling it are pernicious.

Palena Neale suggested that: 'Self-care begins with you. It comes in many shapes and sizes, but done consciously and consistently, it gives you the tools you need to become a better leader and a happier, healthier person.'[82]

---

82 P Neale, '"Serious" leaders need self-care, too' (*Harvard Business Review*, 22 October 2020), https://hbr.org/2020/10/serious-leaders-need-self-care-too, accessed 1 November 2024

We believe leaders should start by slowing down and making time to identify their priorities, working out what they need to become great versions of themselves. Prioritising this for our wellbeing is a valid reason in itself. Additionally, when we deliberately invest time in self-improvement, the benefits ripple out far beyond just us.

The 'self' we mean is the part of you that:

- Finds purpose in what you do
- Appreciates the strengths and gifts you have and wants to use them positively
- Recognises your limits and is kind about them
- Wants to fulfil your potential
- Sees and supports the potential of others

This is the self that, if you protect, nourish and look after it, can accomplish wonderful things, overcome obstacles, keep life and work in perspective, enjoy your moments of success and learn from disappointments. The self that, when at its best, is a positive presence and a contributor.

By legitimising time for yourself as a key leadership practice, we predict that those around you will start to notice your clarity of vision, your enhanced productivity and your capacity to encourage the best in others. This approach can cultivate thriving relationships and openness to new ideas and innovation, as well as resilience during challenging and disruptive times.

It's stirring stuff!

There is one more obstacle to overcome, though. It's one thing to be convinced of your right to proper self-ishness, and it's another to make it a regular and sustained habit. This brings us to:

Tension 3: The practical factor

I know, I know, I know; but I don't have time to do the things that will really make a difference.

At first glance, before breaking away from her record company, Raye was a success. She was writing songs for superstars, collaborating and performing on hit records, yet the one thing that she felt would define her as an artist – her own album – remained out of reach. She had the material ready and had been honing her skills since childhood. However, it wasn't until she sent her 'I'm done' tweet and broke out of the system she was caught in and took control that she was able to fulfil her real potential.

When starting to spend time on ourselves, a significant challenge is identifying practical actions that are suitable and accessible for us. While we might dream of indulging in activities we love – spending time with close friends, visiting a beautiful place, setting out on adventures, learning something new – doing these daily or even weekly isn't always feasible. Instead, we should focus on smaller, manageable moments for ourselves that can fit into our daily routines. This calls for self-awareness and experimentation.

You might not have time for a luxe spa treatment every morning, but taking a moment to breathe and gaze out of the window, or scheduling short walks between meetings, can make a difference. Preferences vary widely, and there's no one-size-fits-all solution. The abundance of choices can be overwhelming, leading to indecision and feelings of guilt or self-consciousness.

Take a few minutes to reflect on what works best for you, no matter how small. These consistent, small habits of investing in yourself can help recharge your energy without taking up much time. Don't forget to occasionally treat yourself as well to guilt-free moments of indulgence that can be both joyful and energising for days afterwards.

When we challenge the stereotypes and clichés of what a leader should look like (someone who performs tirelessly, often without preparation, and is expected to go above and beyond without rest?) and of what time for yourself is (a euphemism for laziness, abdication of responsibility, mystical woowoo?) and instead take a clear-headed look at the possibilities, the neglect of self becomes unwise and unsustainable.

It's important to remember that you have the power to act and prioritise yourself. While, logically, we probably know we shouldn't allow obstacles to get in the way, the reality is that we do. That's often due to a lack of clarity about – or belief in – the achievable actions that *can* make a significant difference.

Paying attention to yourself means taking small, immediate steps with big, long-term benefits – not just for you but for others too. When you give yourself permission to spend time on yourself, you enable those around you to do the same while, in the process, fostering a positive work environment that's productive, safe to be in, innovative and effective.

Without recharging, it becomes impossible to sustain the pace that busyness demands. It is akin to refuelling (or recharging) your car during a long drive. It's essential for replenishing your energy so you can continue on your path effectively.

How exactly do we put the brakes on and locate the charger? We will address that in our next chapter. Before we do so, lets return to Jo's story from the start of this chapter.

For Jo, a personal tragedy – the loss of a loved one to a health-related issue – became a turning point. It forced Jo to confront the neglect of self and wellbeing. Under the weight of grief, a new resolve took root: change achieved through small, consistent steps.

The next morning brought a walk. It wasn't much, but it was a start. Over the next year, these small steps became a habit. Simple exercises were added to the routine, reclaiming health one piece at a time. Jo took increasing control of the work schedule, prioritising time blocks that were carved out for self, not just for work.

The impact was undeniable. Jo's increased energy allowed for longer, more productive workdays. Improved sleep brought a renewed sense of focus and clarity. These changes rippled outwards, creating a positive impact at home as well. Jo had more patience and energy for family, friends and other interests in life. The early steps became a continuous process, one small act paving the way for the next, leading to a more fulfilling life, both professionally and personally.

If nothing else, we hope we've acknowledged in this chapter the complexities involved in prioritising yourself and challenged the misconceptions. Jo's story aptly underscores the fact that time for yourself is not selfish. It is essential for effective leadership.

12
How To Stop The Neglect Of Self

In this final part of the book, we've emphasised the importance of leaders prioritising spending time on themselves. We've delved into the causes and consequences of self-neglect and acknowledged the elusive nature of satisfactory solutions. It's clear that what counts is finding out what works for you and sustaining any changes you want to make, as we'll cover in this chapter.

As we've mentioned, a recurring theme for us has been the notion of the lead single that attracts the most attention from fans and the music industry alike. The track 'Escapism' from *My 21st Century Blues* went viral on TikTok in late 2022 and was a number one in the UK, Denmark and Ireland in 2023, but there was so much more to the album than that. If we're to resolve the challenge of leaders neglecting themselves, we also bump into a big and dominant concept. In this case, it's the term *resilience*.

Defining resilience

Resilience: it's the 'big idea' that we all read about in books, blogs and articles. Or it's the theme of the standout conference speech designed to inspire disaffected business leaders who are looking for a solution; but a solution to what exactly?

When we're not quite sure what lies at the heart of the problem, it's easy to borrow the language that everyone else is using. Before you know it, the common assumption is that we all need to be *resilient* (or be *more* resilient) if we're to remain strong and in control. As a result, both personal and organisational resilience have garnered significant attention, leading to a surge in conversations, expert views and resilience becoming a standard item for leadership development programmes.

Let's go back to basics for a moment. Resilience was previously an engineering term, and it's now applied far more widely to encompass organisations, teams and people as well as materials. It's not just about endurance or being strong – it's also about the capacity to recover after a setback. Organisational resilience is tested by crises (or by risk management and disaster planning, before the worst happens). Perhaps the most recent example this century is how organisations coped during the Covid outbreak, when some struggled due to lack of preparedness, while others transitioned more smoothly.

Looking back to another time of uncertainty, the 2008 financial crisis brought a sharp regulatory focus onto the ability of banks to survive shocks. Now, in looking forward, we see new challenges. Our changing climate, population growth and shrinkage, rapid technology innovation and shifting political attitudes will all test our global, economic, emotional and social resilience. Increasingly, leaders bear the responsibility of building organisations that can adapt to and withstand such extraordinary circumstances. As a direct consequence, there's also increased focus on building *resilient teams* that can function independently; and resilient people, who can stay effective in a relentlessly volatile setting.

In among the fray, there are helpful principles that we can draw from a range of sources. A much-circulated *Harvard Business Review* article, entitled 'Manage your energy, not your time', identified four elements that contribute to effective leadership resilience:

- Physical wellbeing
- Emotional wellbeing

- Mental wellbeing

- Spiritual wellbeing[83]

In addition to this, psychologists have identified a framework that's evolved over time and which encapsulates the key components of resilience. The 7Cs,[84] formulated by Kenneth Ginsberg to support the development of resilience in children, are equally applicable for people in the workplace:

- **Competence:** Recognising what we do well and that we have opportunities to work to those strengths

- **Confidence:** Having belief in our own abilities and experiences

- **Connection:** Forming close ties to family, friends, colleagues and communities

- **Character:** Understanding personal values and ethical responsibilities

- **Contribution:** Having a sense of being useful and valuable to others and being able to ask for help

- **Coping:** Developing problem-solving skills, managing anxiety and letting go

- **Control:** Feeling autonomy over one's life and environment

---

83 T Schwartz and C McCarthy, 'Manage your energy, not your time' (*Harvard Business Review*, October 2007), https://hbr.org/2007/10/manage-your-energy-not-your-time, accessed 1 November 2024

84 K Ginsberg, *The 7 C's Model of Resilience* (Ashland Decisions 2016)

Any of these descriptions can be a starting point or catalyst for reflection on what might help maintain individual resilience. Ultimately, it's about finding what truly makes a difference to each of us, as we seek ways to care for ourselves, remain effective and realise our potential – or discover what brings us happiness and comfort in our own skin.

Inevitably, there are challenges to the prevailing 'resilience orthodoxy', as author and former Head of Twitter (EMEA) Bruce Daisley calls it. In his book *Fortitude*, he proposes that the lazy use of 'being more resilient' as a response to any hardship is misconceived. He questions the idea that individuals are ever resilient, and that true strength and fulfilment come from our shared experience and deep connection with others: 'Fortitude, the strength that we draw from each other and those around us, along with some simple mind exercises can create a more effective pathway to greater self-confidence, inner strength and courage.'[85]

Daisley joins a group of voices that question whether resilience training creates any lasting benefit, especially where organisations take no serious steps to address the systemic drivers of stress, discomfort and pressure in their structures and cultures.

---

85 B Daisley, *Fortitude: The myth of resilience, and the secrets of inner strength* (Penguin, 20 April 2023)

Other critics caution against relying on resilience as a one-size-fits-all solution. They warn that this approach might lead us to overlook genuine threats to our health and wellbeing, to be overly optimistic about the challenges we face, or to set increasingly unrealistic goals that we're unlikely to achieve.

Our view is that the topic of resilience – particularly the Schwartz and McCarthy definitions of physical, emotional, mental and spiritual wellbeing – can help people open useful lines of enquiry.

We've already described our typical resilience exercise with clients that helps people identify what adds to their strength, wellbeing or feeling of resilience and what subtracts from it.

Having completed this thinking, we have two further questions:

1. Which habits could you develop to nurture yourself and boost your resilience?

2. How can you include others to support you in this journey?

Rather than skip past this thinking only to be lost in the rest of your day, why not stop right now and take some time to complete this process. In notes you can return to later, create two columns, headed: *What energises me?* and *What drains me?* Spend time noting anything you can think of in each of the columns, including considering the two questions above. An investment of five minutes now will be worthwhile for you later. This is the first step in identifying what you require to stop neglecting yourself.

Numerous prominent business leaders speak openly about their individual habits and priorities. Deborah Meaden, serial entrepreneur and the first female dragon on the BBCs *Dragons' Den*, has a habitual morning routine:

> 'I get up at half past eight or nine o'clock – I'm a late riser. I have a cup of tea, and then whatever the weather I go outside barefoot into the garden. It's grounding, it reminds me what is important in life, and it's a moment of stillness.'[86]

Grace Lordan, writing in the *Financial Times* in August 2023, tried out a number of CEOs' morning routines, almost all of which included some sort of physical exercise:

> 'I experimented with a myriad of exercise options post meditation. These included boxing, horseback riding, jogging, the martial art Krav Maga, Pilates, swimming and yoga.

86 D Greenwell, 'Life lessons: Deborah Meaden on what life has taught her' (Positive.News, 10 March 2023), www.positive.news/society/life-lessons-deborah-meaden-on-what-life-has-taught-her, accessed 1 November 2024

For me, the winner ended up being stretching and a long walk.'[87]

You may find any of these options appealing or appalling. Perhaps you know what you need already; or maybe an experimental phase to discover what really works for you might be a useful step. For us, the crucial moment is when you decide that identifying what you need is a valuable, worthwhile and legitimate use of your time.

Having made the decision to locate what works for you, the next step is turning your investment in yourself into a lasting practice – not just a fleeting tune you momentarily enjoy but soon forget. It's time to master the art of forming good habits.

As humans we possess an instinctive understanding of what adjustments we need to make in our lives to be at our best. We already recognise the activities that energise us, even though we might lack the space to reflect on them. Many of us will make our New Year's resolutions that then drift off course in mid-February. It's the same disparity between intention and action that we frequently encounter in our work. We see many individuals desire change but struggle to sustain it over time.

---

87   G Lordan, 'Starting the day like Jamie Dimon set me up for success' (*Financial Times*, 28 August 2023), www.ft.com/content/7e47ff11-e533-490f-9286-54ad628aac08, accessed 1 November 2024

The solution lies in how we can structure and consciously engineer small, seemingly inconsequential, daily and weekly habits that can compound to deliver better results and over time make what seems impossible a reality.

The anatomy of habits

It's our conviction that the long-term answer to the neglect of self lies in our repeated habits.

We challenge the common misconception that habits are achieved through self-motivation. Instead, we'd argue that they thrive on structure and process. Motivation may kickstart a habit initially, but without the right framework, the motivation will likely fade. In his book *Atomic Habits*, James Clear outlines the anatomy of habit succinctly:

- **The cue:** a trigger that prompts a behaviour, which could be a desire for relaxation leading to a craving for something sweet

- **The craving itself:** the internal motivation to change one's state, whether it's hunger, coldness or emotional fulfilment

- **The response:** the action taken to satisfy the craving, like reaching for a snack or accepting a meeting invite

- **The reward:** the satisfaction of the craving, whether it's feeling full, warm or valued[88]

After a while, this forms a habit loop and becomes automatic, in some cases without any conscious thought. Take the example of feeling a little cold (cue). Without much conscious thought, we realise we want to be warm (craving), so we reach for a sweater or dial up the heating (response), and then we become warm (reward).

We learn from this series of loops, and over time the behaviour becomes embedded as a habit.

We acknowledge and celebrate the importance of James Clear's work as a valuable resource for further exploration.

The process that we recommend – for forming good habits – takes his work as its starting point and then maps a step-by-step route to embedding better habits for yourself.

How to embed new habits

Our three-stage process for creating and sustaining lasting habits invites you to work through three steps, as illustrated and explained below.

---

88 J Clear, *Atomic Habits: An easy & proven way to build good habits & break bad ones* (Avery, 2018)

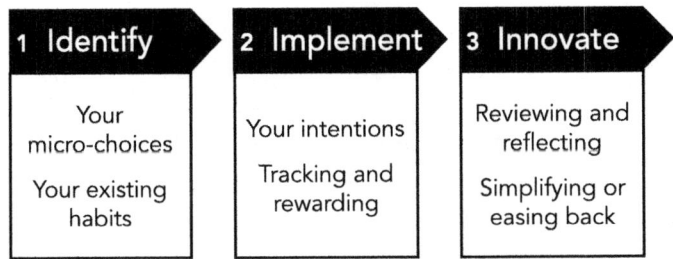

Embedding better habits

1. Identify

In establishing a habit that contributes to effective time for yourself, the first step is to identify:

- Your micro-choices
- Your existing habits
- Your habit-stacking opportunities

Micro-choices – the countless minor decisions you make without thinking – have the potential to create substantial impact over time and yet require minimal effort, cost or risk. For instance, you might opt to wear your favourite clothes while working from home to lift your mood, rather than keeping them locked away in the wardrobe except for special occasions. You might decide to start the morning by dropping a colleague a note to say how much you appreciated something they did the previous day, rather than simply diving into your emails and reacting to immediate events. Even dedicating just one minute a day, every day, to mindful breathing instead of venting frustrations to a team member can deliver significant change over time.

By incorporating subtle yet intentional actions into your daily routine, you harness the power of your micro-choices, amplifying their cumulative effect and fostering positive habits for long-term development and growth.

Various internet sources suggest that we make between 33,000 and 35,000 choices each day, many of which we do automatically with little thought. Optimising just a small number of those can give you better outcomes and create more energy in your day.[89]

To spot the possibilities, try creating your own habit audit using personal audit tables like those outlined below. Reflect on your typical days, from waking to bedtime, and take note of these routines.

Hourly audit

	MON	TUE	WED	THU	FRI	SAT	SUN
06.00							
07.00							
08.00							
09.00							
10.00							

89 A Reill, 'A simple way to make better decisions' (*Harvard Business Review*, 5 December 2023), https://hbr.org/2023/12/a-simple-way-to-make-better-decisions, accessed 2 November 2024

	MON	TUE	WED	THU	FRI	SAT	SUN
11.00							
12.00							
13.00							
14.00							
15.00							
16.00							
17.00							
18.00							
19.00							
20.00							
21.00							
22.00							
23.00							

Daily audit

	MORNING	AFTERNOON	EVENING
MONDAY			
TUESDAY			
WEDNESDAY			
THURSDAY			
FRIDAY			
SATURDAY			
SUNDAY			

Document the habits you engage in daily and/or weekly. Some of these habits will be conscious, while others may occur automatically. You might be surprised by what you discover.

Once you've gathered your personal audit data, look for the opportunities to integrate new or refined habits. When adopting a new habit, linking it to an existing, effortless routine can serve as an automatic reminder – a strategy known as *habit stacking* – and make it easier to do. For instance, to incorporate the habit of learning from recent experience, you could schedule time in the last ten minutes of your lunch break. By allocating a specific time – say, between 12.50 and 13.00 every day – to reflect on a recent incident and draw out helpful insight, you capitalise on the habitual nature of your lunchtime itself. Identify:

1. **Your micro-choices**

- Remember you are more powerful than you think you are.

- Remember that these are numerous, small, discretionary everyday choices.

- While the effort, cost and risk involved are minimal, cumulatively they deliver high impact, shaping the course of your life.

2. **Your existing habits**

- List the habits that you repeat each day or each week, some of which you will be conscious of, others not so.

- Think of a typical day, from waking to going to bed, listing each habit alongside the time you do it. You may be surprised at what you find.

3. **Your habit-stacking opportunities**

- From your list of daily or weekly habits, identify opportunities to attach your new desired habits to existing ones. This way you use a ready-made cue.

CASE STUDY: New tunes

Catrina is a lifelong music fan and describes listening to music as essential for her wellbeing, creativity, balance and happiness. She found herself, though, relying on familiar and favourite music that she could access without thinking, and not taking time to explore new, different or diverse artists. Given the multiplicity of choices available, she was also unsure where to start. The options seemed overwhelming, and there never seemed to be enough time.

She decided to take action when her Spotify app showed her the top five artists she had listened to in the previous twelve months. The list was exactly the same as the year before!

One of Catrina's consistent, non-negotiable habits is doing *The New York Times* Wordle each morning with a cup of tea. She experimented with the idea of listening to a new song each time she did the Wordle (or two, depending on how challenging it was).

She now has a playlist of artists and songs that she adds to throughout the course of any given week. She gathers these through recommendations, reading, different media and pure chance, so there is always a song waiting each morning. Even after a few weeks, she was amazed at how rich, satisfying and inspiring her new musical habit was.

This deliberate intention setting leads us to our next stage.

2. Implement

In addition to the practice of habit stacking, where you commit to *After [existing habit X], I will do [new habit Y]*, there are two other tools to help you implement your new habits:

- Implementation intentions
- Tracking and rewarding

Implementation intentions

Based on the work of Peter Gollwitzer and Paschal Sheeran, we recommend *implementation intentions* to enhance habit adoption.[90]

---

90 PM Gollwitzer and P Sheeran, 'Implementation intentions and goal achievement: A meta-analysis of effects and processes', *Advances in Experimental Social Psychology*, 38 (2006), 69–119, https://doi.org/10.1016/S0065-2601(06)38002-1

Implementation intentions involve explicitly stating what you intend to do, when you intend to do it and where. Research suggests that by consciously specifying what they intend to do, individuals can increase their chances of following through by approximately 50%. This has been extensively studied, particularly in the realm of exercise science with both experienced and less frequent exercisers.[91]

Committing to actions such as *I will take a break from my desk and go for a walk at 12.00pm every day* significantly enhances the likelihood of success. By anchoring the behaviour to a specific time and place, we establish clear action, emphasise accountability and increase the likelihood of sticking with it. We would encourage you to express your implementation by behaviour, time and location:

I will [behaviour/action] at [time] in [location].

Tracking

Once you have committed to an implementation intention in writing, you can decide how you will track and reward yourself. You might use an app, a desktop tracker, an Excel sheet, a habit journal, a diary or your Outlook calendar – whatever provides you with a simple way to monitor your efforts. It doesn't

---

91 S Milne et al., 'Combining motivational and volitional interventions to promote exercise participation: Protection motivation theory and implementation intentions', *British Journal of Health Psychology*, 7/2 (2002), 163–84, https://doi.org/10.1348/135910702169420

matter how you track; the important part is the tracking itself.

Engaging in this tracking process serves two purposes:

1. It signals that you value the habit enough to actively monitor it (significant from both a neuroscience perspective and an adoption perspective).

2. It allows you to reflect on your progress.

The figure below gives an example of a habit-tracking template.

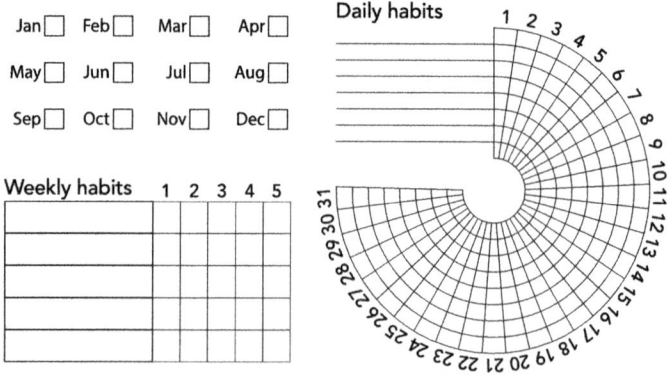

Leadership habit tracker

Rewarding

Happily, it's crucial to incorporate rewards into your habit-building. Rewarding yourself after completing a habit can reinforce its adoption.

Rewarding yourself is personal. Choose small gestures or actions that celebrate your success in making space for yourself. It's crucial to pick rewards that match what you're aiming for. For instance, if you're trying to improve your health, eating a Mars bar after an exercise session wouldn't help! It's important to think this through to avoid undermining your efforts.

Perhaps you can see yourself rewarded with a good cup of coffee after reading a chapter of a book each day. Or you might find it satisfying to mark off completed tasks in a habit journal. For those who like something more tactile, adding a marble to a jar for each positive interaction with a team member can be fulfilling.

Finding the perfect rewards might require some trial and error, but it's key to reinforcing your habits. It gives you that dopamine boost that helps solidify your routines.

3. Innovate

This final third step is to innovate by:

- Reviewing and reflecting
- Simplifying or easing back

Reviewing and reflecting

Dan Pink's book, *Drive*, concludes that mastery is one of the three significant motivators of human beings.[92] We love getting better at what we do, and innovation is achieved through regular review and time for reflection.

At the end of each month:

- Step back and review your progress.

- Reflect on your successes, the obstacles you've faced and their potential causes.

- Look for any recurring patterns or trends that can guide you in maintaining consistency or building on your accomplishments.

A selection of questions we find useful to reflect on are as follows:

- What was your most significant achievement last month, and which factors led to it?

- What goals did you set but didn't reach?

- What obstacles prevented you from achieving those goals?

---

92 DH Pink, *Drive: The surprising truth about what motivates us* (Canongate Books, 2018)

- If you could begin the month again, knowing what you know now, what advice would you give yourself?

- What lessons have you learned and what actions will you take into the next month?

Simplifying or easing back

One client found that reading a chapter from a leadership book at the end of the workday wasn't effective, even though they scheduled it in their calendar. They decided to switch things up by reading for fifteen minutes before starting work each day. This small change led to a consistent habit, and over six months, they completed four books, contributing to substantial personal growth.

This process of reflection allows you to adapt and make the necessary adjustments, which is crucial for forming lasting habits. One common reason people give up on their New Year's resolutions or struggle with new patterns of behaviour is setting overly ambitious goals from the start. Surprisingly, scaling back to more attainable goals can increase consistency and long-term commitment.

For example, instead of aiming to exercise for thirty minutes three times a week to clear your mind, you could start with a ten-minute walk once or twice a week. Starting with smaller, achievable tasks and gradually increasing them helps build the habit more effectively and ensures its sustainability over time.

It is also important to acknowledge that no single day, week or month is identical to another. We've explored extensively how unpredictable and volatile working life can be, and instead of completely dropping the regular habits that rejuvenate us, it can be more beneficial to scale them down. Maintaining momentum is key to sustaining change.

Innovation is often assumed to apply only to major shifts or transformations. However, when it comes to habits personal to you, the most impactful innovations are often subtle. For instance, if our client had simply abandoned the goal of reading a chapter from a book instead of adjusting the time and duration, they would have missed out on the benefits of completing those four leadership books.

In this chapter our aim has been to encourage you to give yourself permission to prioritise yourself. To take a practical step towards proper selfishness.

With the relentless pace of modern work and life, for the busy leader simply pushing through until the next holiday isn't sufficient. Operating in a suboptimal state for weeks on end can lead to poor decision making, dislocation from colleagues and potential burnout.

Let's remind ourselves that it's perfectly acceptable for leaders to allocate time solely for themselves. By doing so, they equip themselves to handle critical situations and interactions with clarity and composure, and in alignment with their values. This dedicated time allows them to optimise their effectiveness, ensuring they approach difficult moments with a clear mind, self-awareness, compassion and readiness for empathy.

We also emphasise that investing in personal wellbeing generates a greater likelihood of enjoying your moments of achievement, relishing what you do, and reawakening a personal sense of purpose and excitement, not to mention the positive light you might shine on other people.

While there may be a backlash against traditional approaches to resilience training, we would still consider understanding what works for you as a fundamental aspect of caring for yourself. The most effective solutions emerge when individuals can think independently and tailor their own approaches towards time for self.

Once we know what we need to do, we can consciously work on the habits that replenish us on a consistent basis, rather than relying solely on occasional breaks or ideal circumstances that may never materialise.

Ultimately, we all need to recognise that we don't need perfect conditions to make a start. Your first step can be as small as you like, as long as you take the next small step and the next. Five minutes spent today, tomorrow and next week on yourself can yield significant benefits, and that simple act alone can be deeply empowering.

There's no time like now. Are you ready?

Conclusion

Before you chose to read this book, you may have been experiencing frustration, concern or confusion about your leadership practice. We hope that we have helped you connect to a refreshed sense of clarity and purpose. You might even have your diary open, ready to clear out its unnecessary clutter and make time for new, leadership-enhancing habits.

Think about Air's deliberate approach with *Moon Safari*. Next time you're faced with pressure to act, take a moment to step back, make space for thoughtful deliberation, and aim for a distinctive and compelling course of action that's both effective and underpinned with quality decision making.

The next time you have to set up a new team, find ways to work with new people, or navigate a project that brings uncertainty or ambiguity, we hope you'll think Bowie and spend time together with others, curious about what makes each other tick and establishing lasting trust.

Perhaps you'll be inspired by Raye and take on challenging situations without losing sight of yourself. Rather than reacting reflexively or trying to make everyone else happy, take the time to assess your needs and capabilities too so that you can truly excel in any circumstance.

We have outlined opportunities for action in this book to help address the neglect of fundamental leadership principles. If you choose to take action, you'll make some significant discoveries about yourself, about the people you work with, and about the difference that amazing leaders can make. We've certainly seen our clients, their people and businesses flourish when they've adopted the principles and habits we've set out in these pages.

Like our inspirational musicians, you're not on your own. We're only too happy to hear from you and offer additional resources. Head over to our website, where you'll find a variety of free-to-download tools, such as our Habit Calendar, and other material designed to support you: www.oxford-group.com/neglected-acts-of-leadership

For now, though, sit back and breathe. You have taken the first step simply by taking the time to read this book. That's an accomplishment in itself, and it will help you on the path towards professional growth and personal understanding.

That might seem like the easy part, but the rest needn't be complicated or overly demanding if you take it step by step. We're confident that some of the biggest impacts you'll experience in stopping the neglect will be the result of the small acts of leadership you choose to make.

Acknowledgements

This book simply would not have been possible without the shared wisdom, experience and passion of our team of coaches, consultants and colleagues at The Oxford Group, and of our clients and their leaders around the globe. We are united in our belief that leadership matters.

Finally, thank you for taking your time to read this book. We hope it helps you to create the conditions for your future leadership success.

The Authors

Andy Dent

 An experienced consultant and coach, Andy has an engaging, pragmatic and action-orientated approach to working with individuals and teams to change mindsets, shift behaviour and exceed business and personal goals at all levels of leadership.

Andy joined The Oxford Group in 2018. He has held several roles, including director of Solutions, Innovation and People and, most recently, sales director.

In his earlier career, Andy was in health club management with Virgin Active/Esporta and David Lloyd.

Following this, he held senior management and directorship posts within training organisations, then spent five years with The Institute of Leadership and Management (a City & Guilds business) before joining The Oxford Group.

Andy is passionate about helping leaders and organisations embed habits, mindsets and conditions that lead to high performance.

Caroline Taylor

 A highly experienced and authentic executive leader, coach and organisational development consultant, Caroline has more than three decades of expertise in working with global organisations across various sectors and geographies. Throughout her career, she has successfully led on leadership development; talent management; executive succession; equity, diversity and inclusion (EDI); talent acquisition; performance management; employee engagement; and organisational change initiatives.

Caroline is passionate about creating long-lasting impact and empowering leaders to develop their individual capabilities while enhancing their leadership agility. Her focus is on supporting leaders in navigating and driving change effectively in today's dynamic environments.

Since 2022 she has served as the managing director of The Oxford Group – a global leadership development consultancy acquired by City & Guilds in 2015 – and holds executive director responsibility for Leadership Development Solutions across City & Guilds.

Catrina Hewitson

 A consultant, facilitator, team coach and long-standing associate of The Oxford Group, Catrina has sophisticated, global, cross-sectoral experience in working with leaders. Her body of work includes strategy and strategic implementation, innovative leadership programmes and interventions, and helping teams work towards their highest potential.

Catrina believes that leaders benefit from accessing the richest sources of inspiration, best practice and ideas. She draws from history, philosophy, business, art, music and contemporary culture in her approach to development.

She loves helping people find their confidence, voice, courage and purpose.

An experienced non-executive, she has held board roles in heritage, housing and arts organisations.

🌐 www.oxford-group.com

🔗 www.linkedin.com/company/the-oxford-group

Printed in Dunstable, United Kingdom